to dance

To Mom, for supporting my passion, and
To Mark, for helping me tell it
—S. C. S.

To Richard Jackson, my Captain
—M. S.

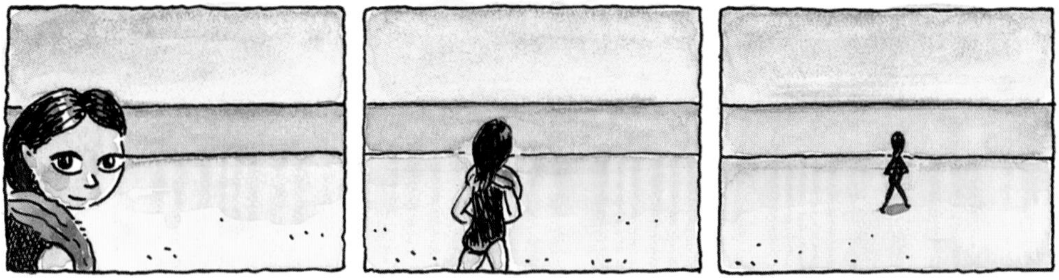

to dance

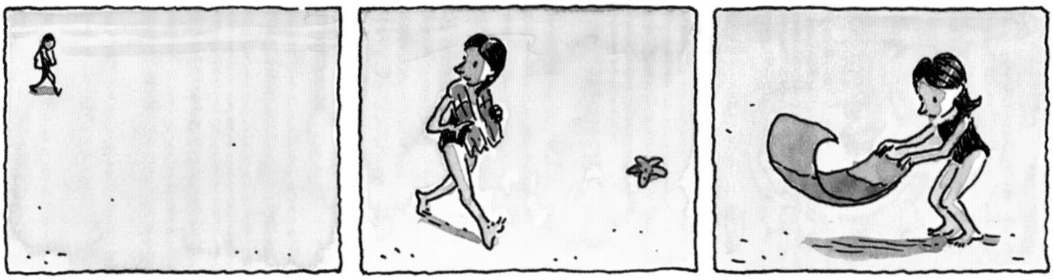

a memoir by Siena Cherson Siegel

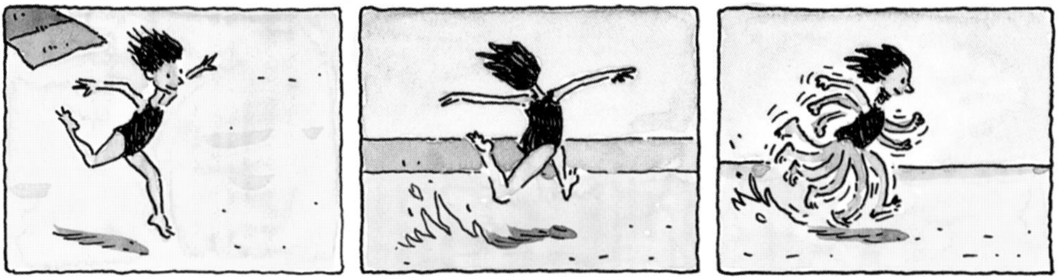

with artwork by Mark Siegel

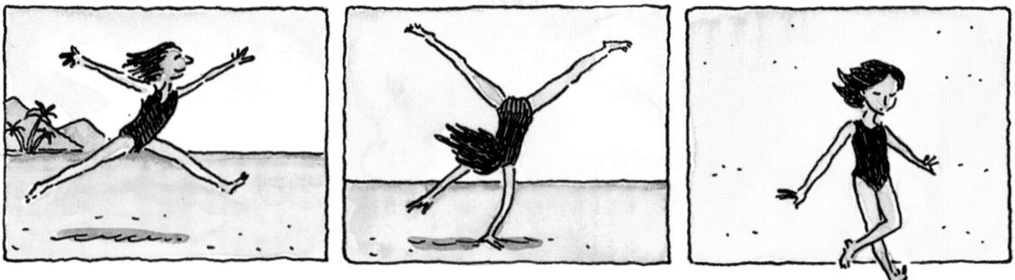

Atheneum Books for Young Readers New York London Toronto Sydney New Delhi

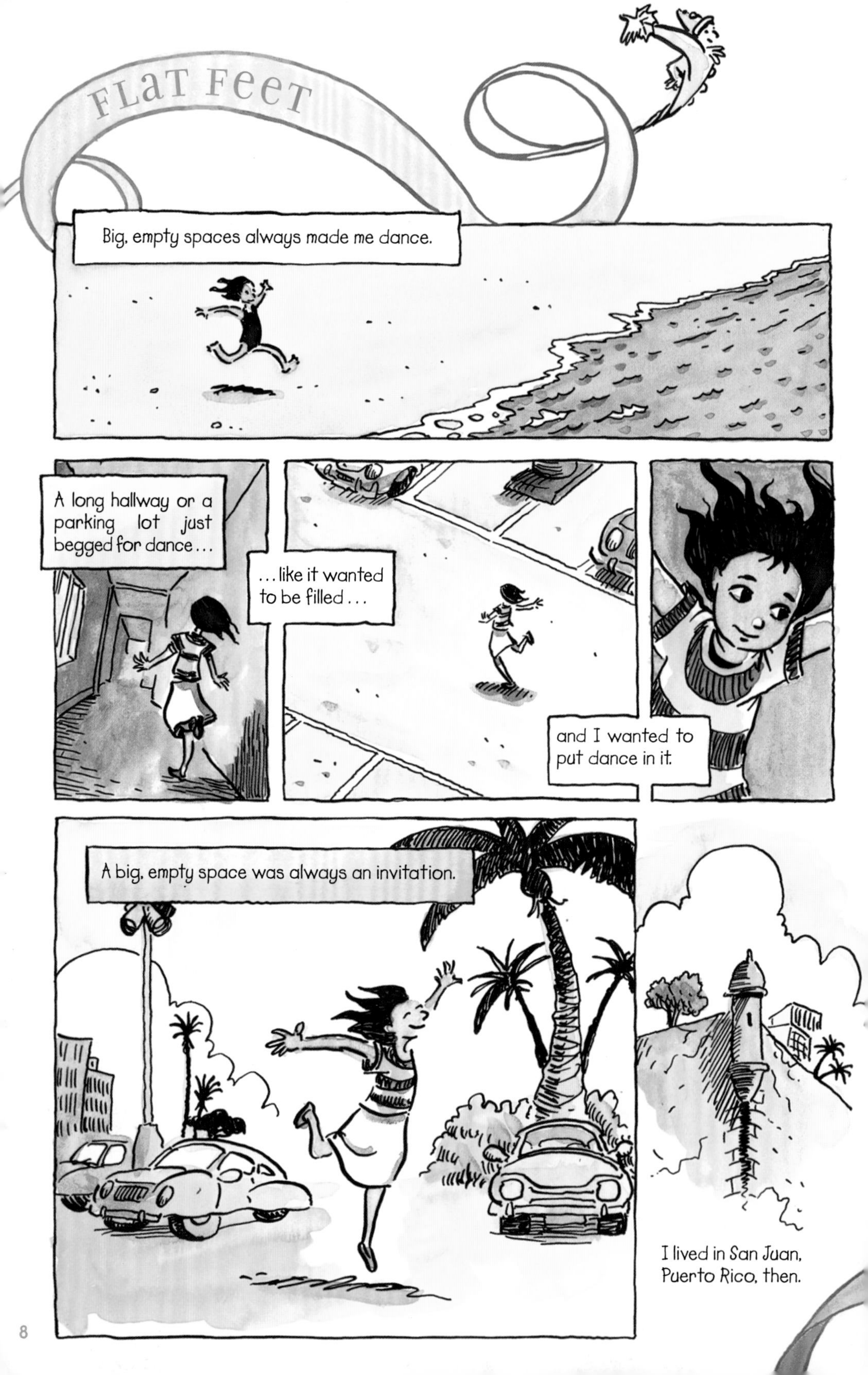
Flat Feet
Big, empty spaces always made me dance.
A long hallway or a parking lot just begged for dance...
...like it wanted to be filled...
and I wanted to put dance in it.
A big, empty space was always an invitation.
I lived in San Juan, Puerto Rico, then.

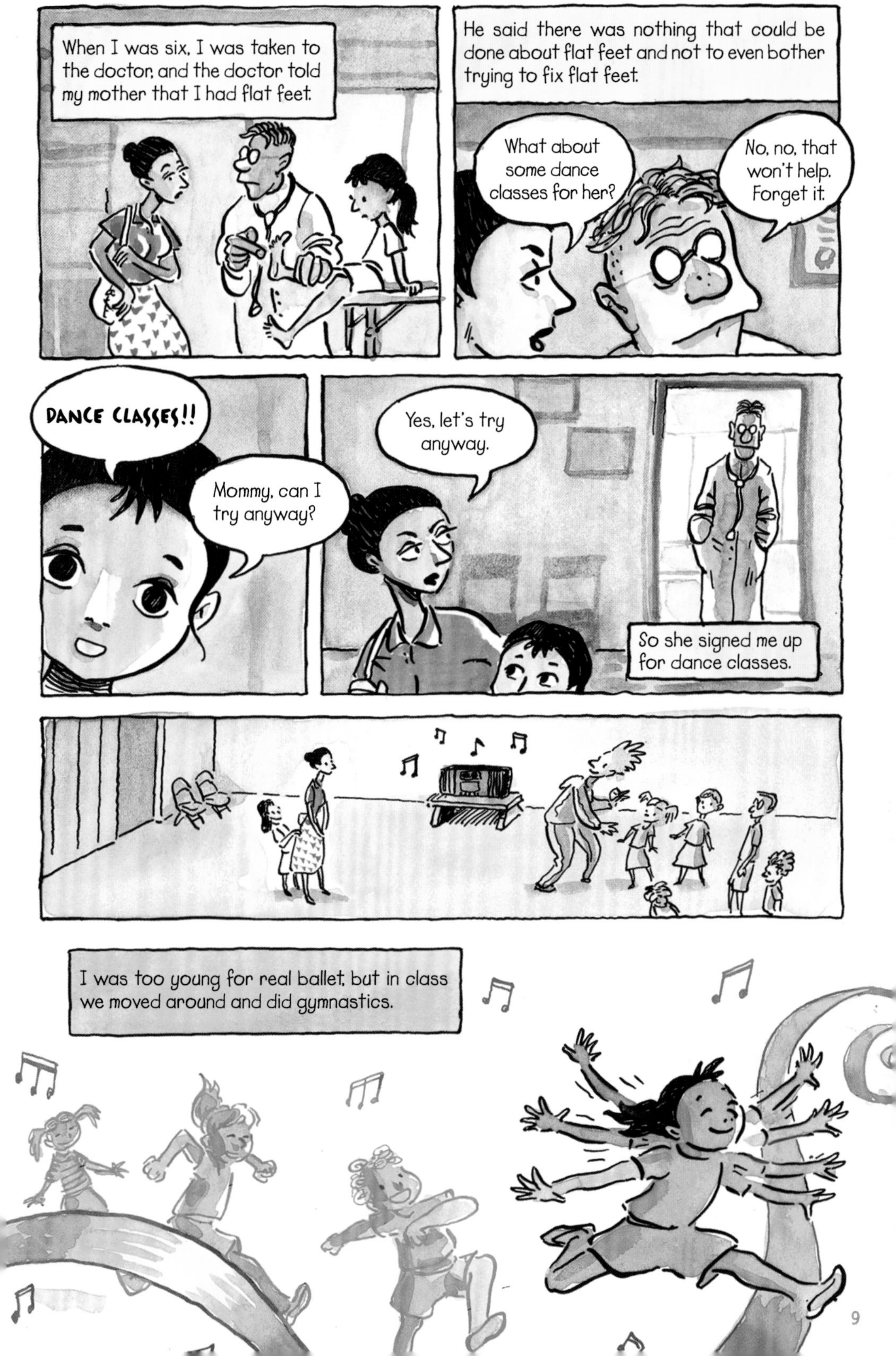

When I was six, I was taken to the doctor, and the doctor told my mother that I had flat feet.
He said there was nothing that could be done about flat feet and not to even bother trying to fix flat feet.
What about some dance classes for her?
No, no, that won't help. Forget it.
DANCE CLASSES!!
Mommy, can I try anyway?
Yes, let's try anyway.
So she signed me up for dance classes.
I was too young for real ballet, but in class we moved around and did gymnastics.

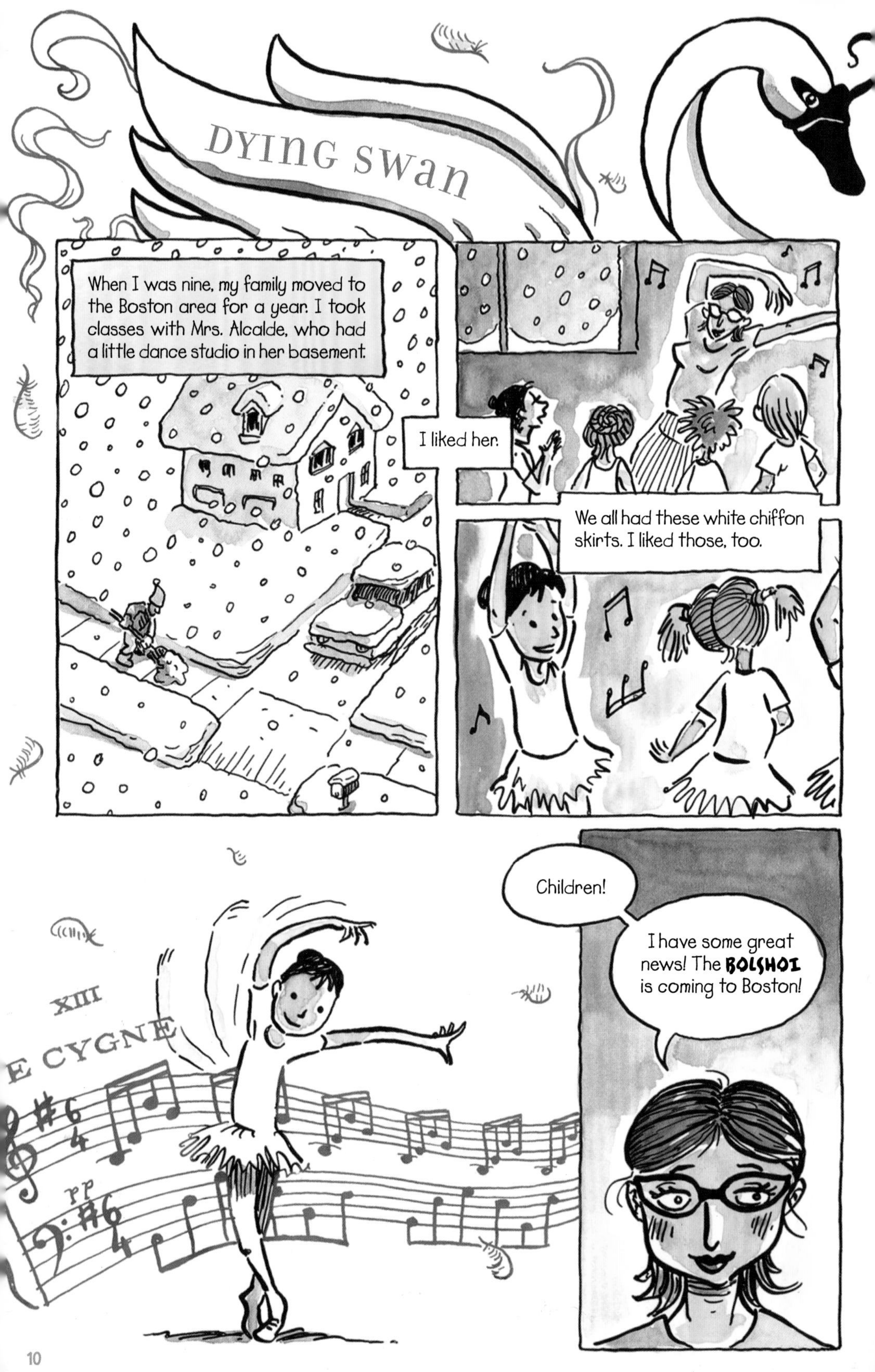
DYING SWAN
When I was nine, my family moved to the Boston area for a year. I took classes with Mrs. Alcalde, who had a little dance studio in her basement.
I liked her.
We all had these white chiffon skirts. I liked those, too.
XIII
E CYGNE
pp
Children!
I have some great news! The BOLSHOI is coming to Boston!

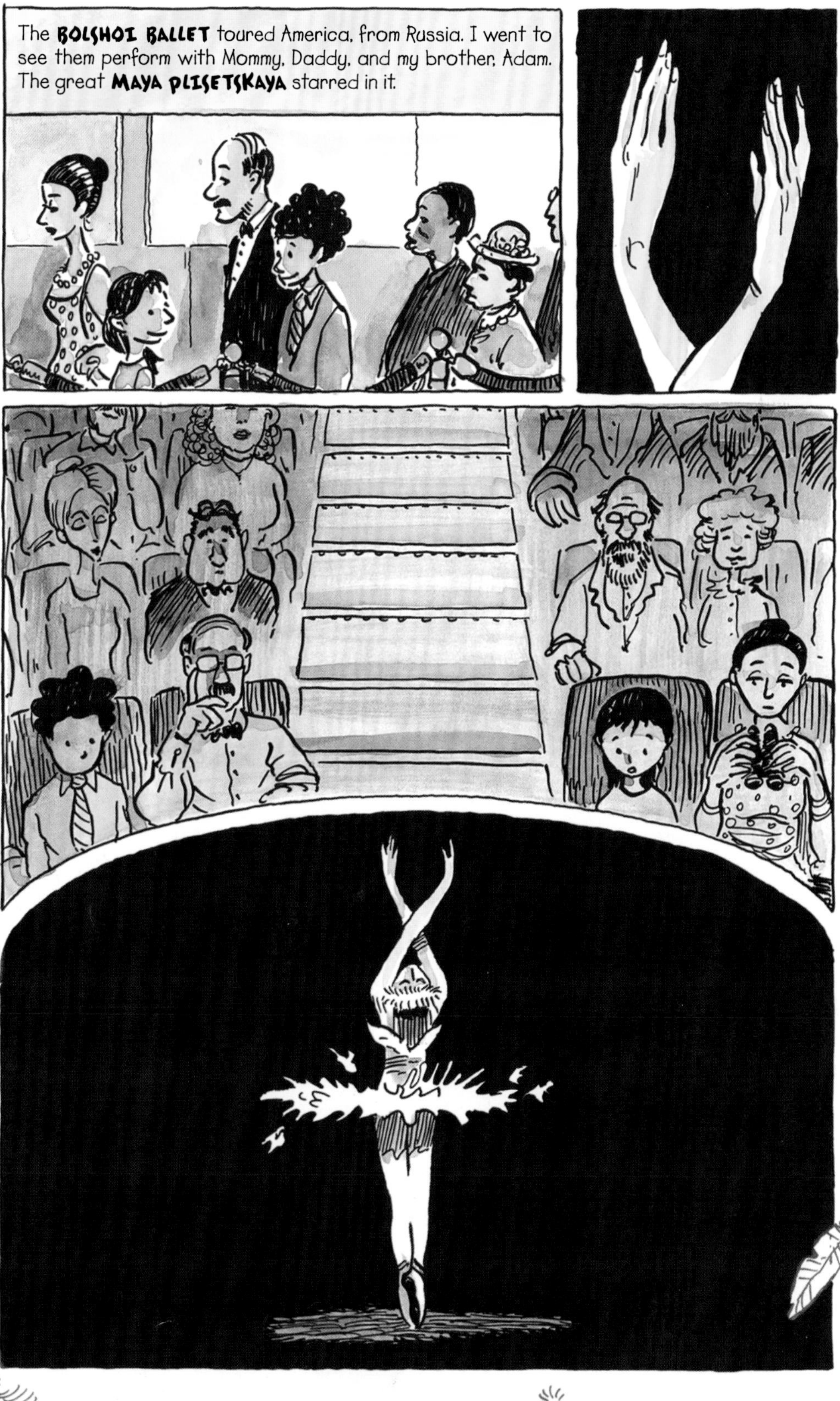
The BOLSHOI BALLET toured America, from Russia. I went to see them perform with Mommy, Daddy, and my brother, Adam. The great MAYA PLISETSKAYA starred in it.

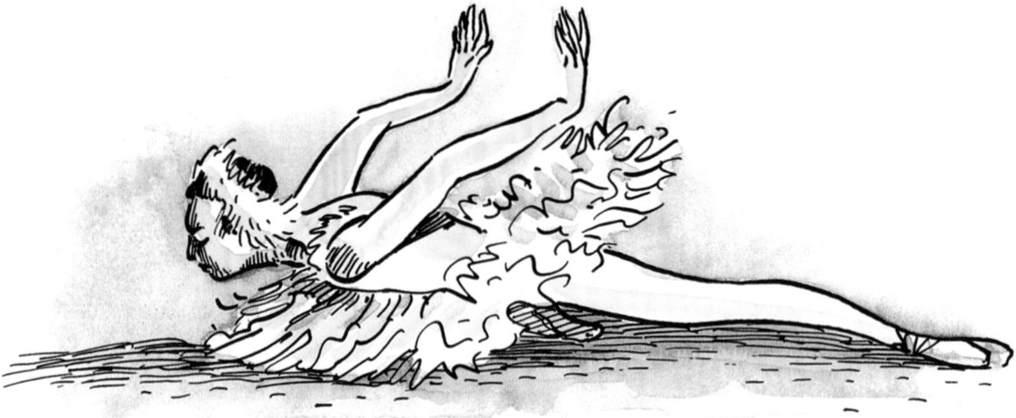

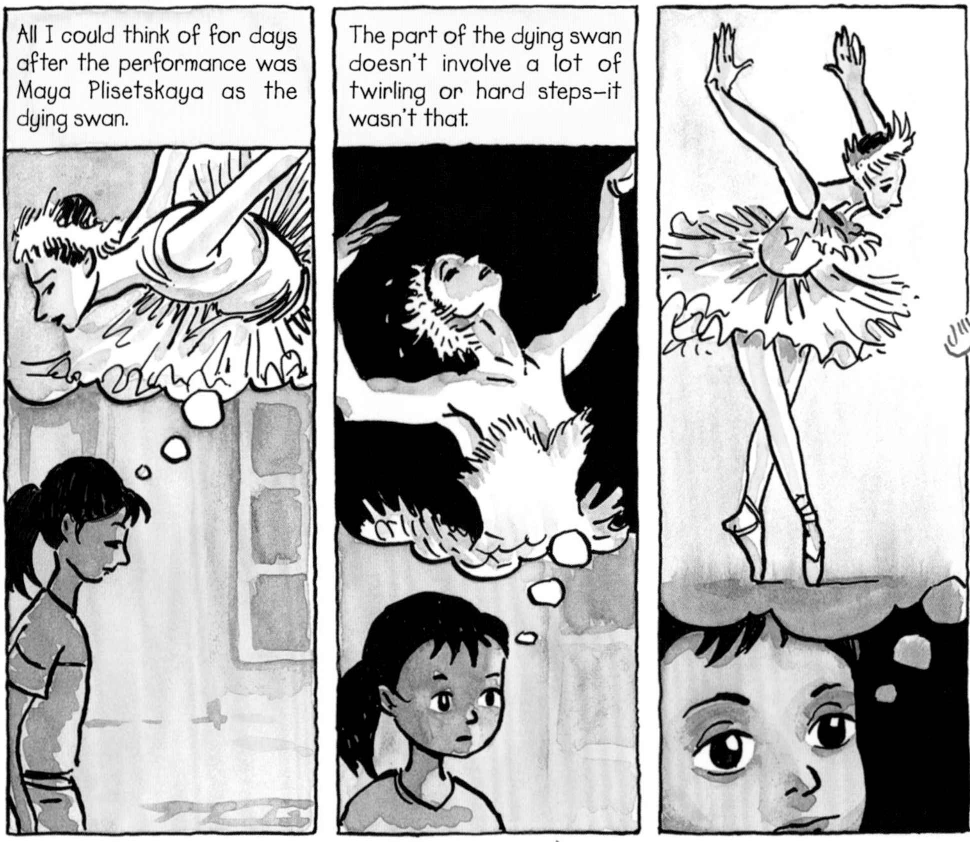
All I could think of for days after the performance was Maya Plisetskaya as the dying swan.
The part of the dying swan doesn't involve a lot of twirling or hard steps—it wasn't that.

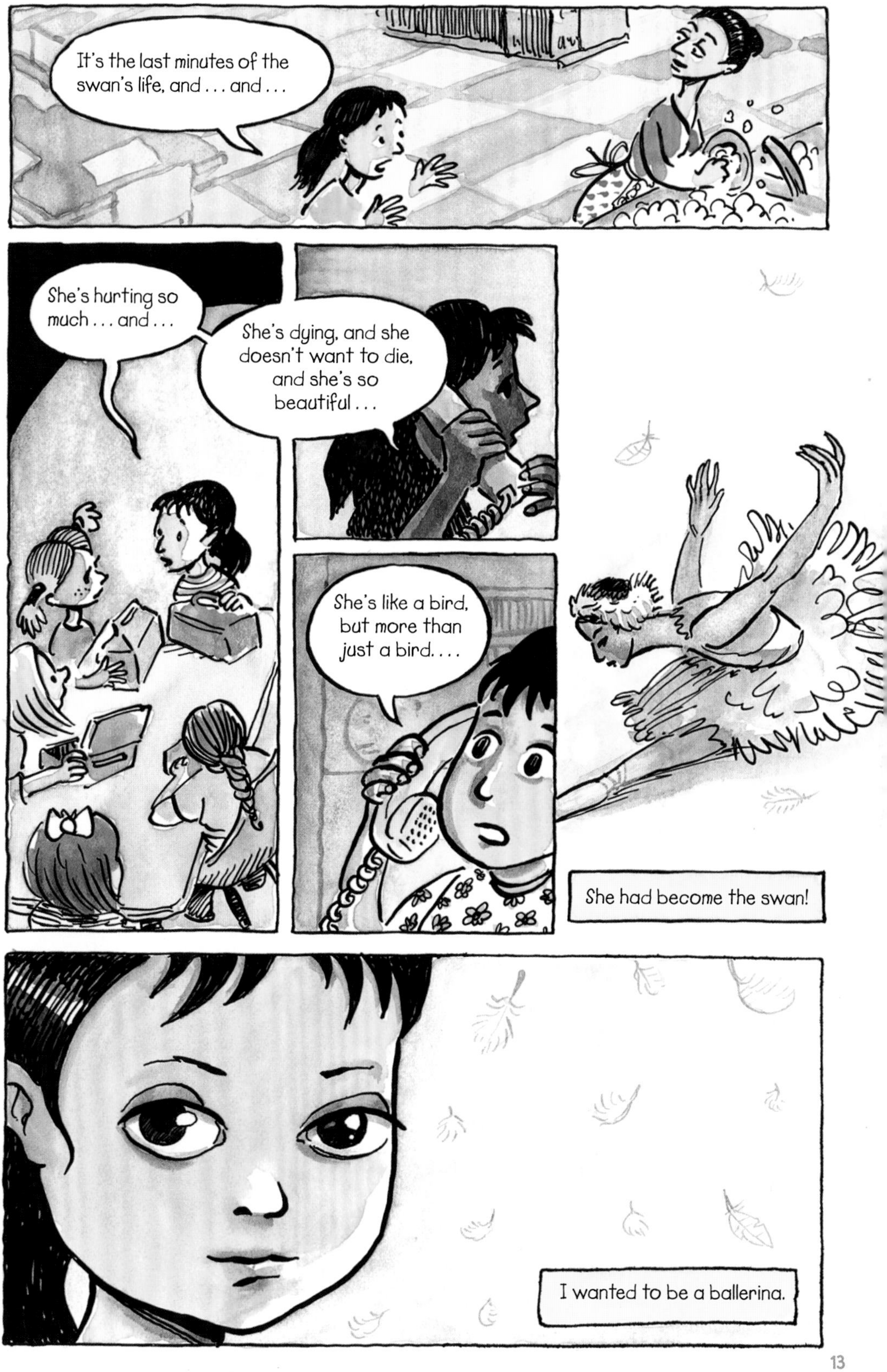
It's the last minutes of the swan's life, and . . . and . . .
She's hurting so much . . . and . . .
She's dying, and she doesn't want to die, and she's so beautiful . . .
She's like a bird, but more than just a bird. . . .
She had become the swan!
I wanted to be a ballerina.

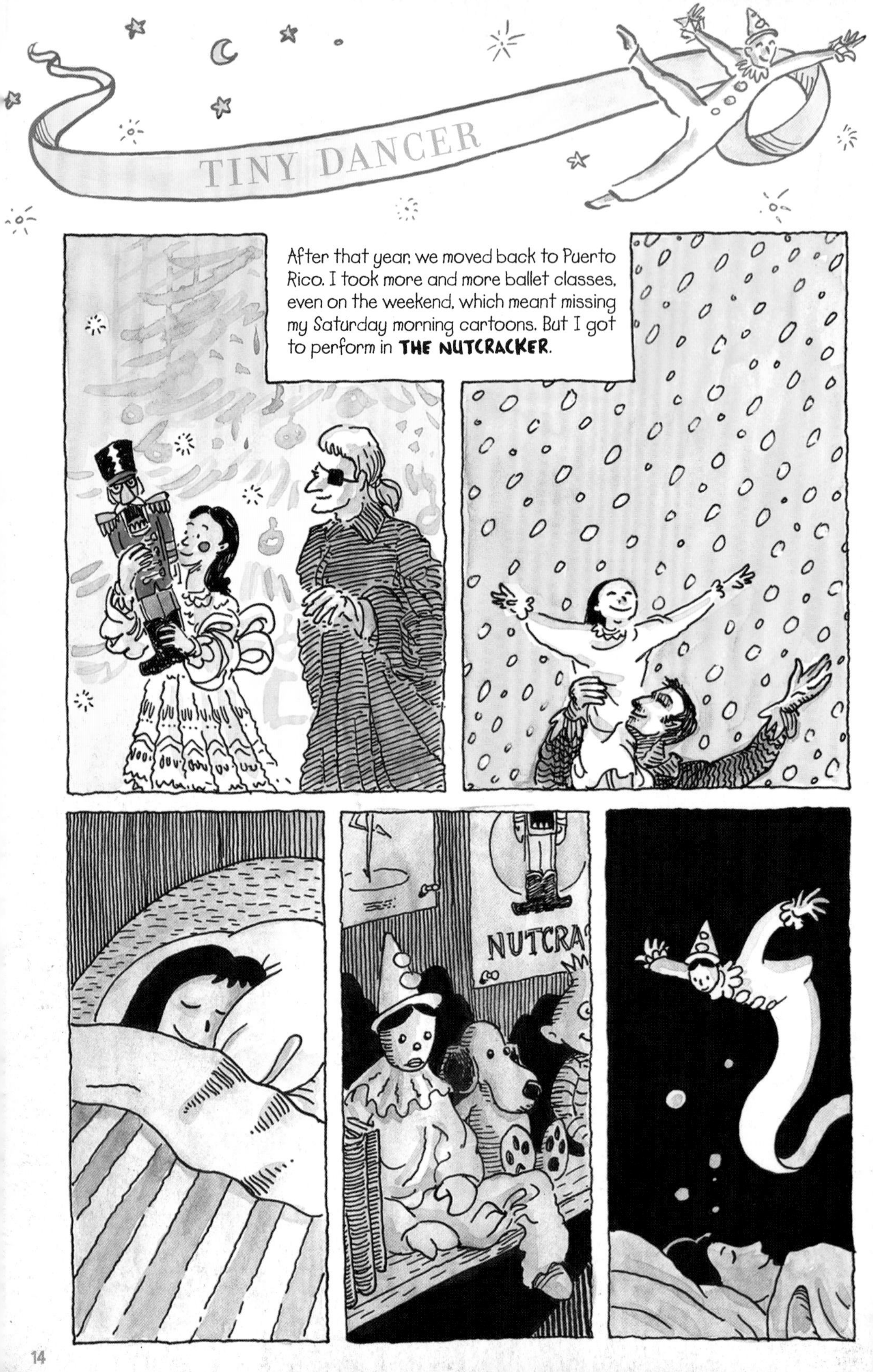
TINY DANCER
After that year, we moved back to Puerto Rico. I took more and more ballet classes, even on the weekend, which meant missing my Saturday morning cartoons. But I got to perform in THE NUTCRACKER.
NUTCRA

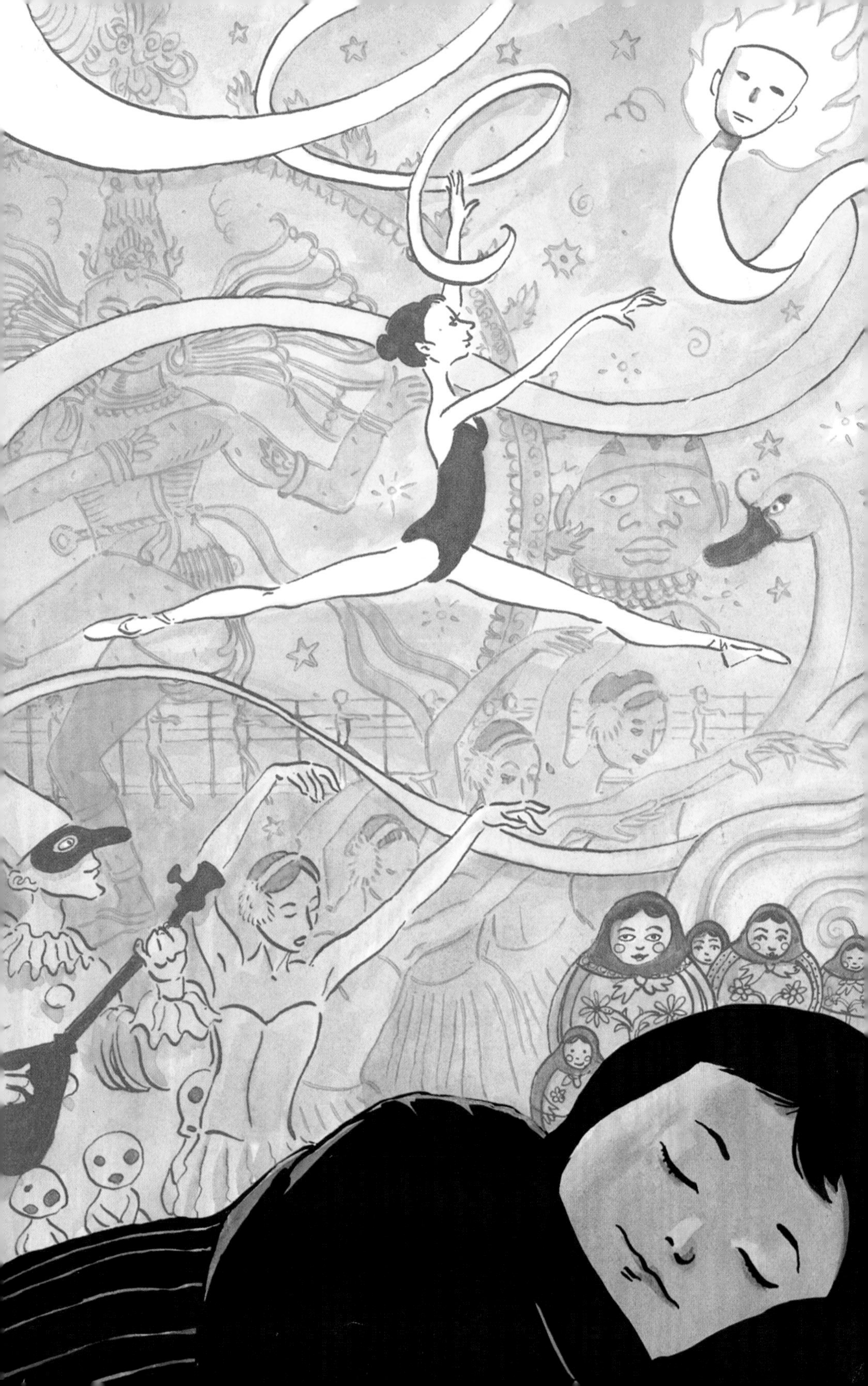

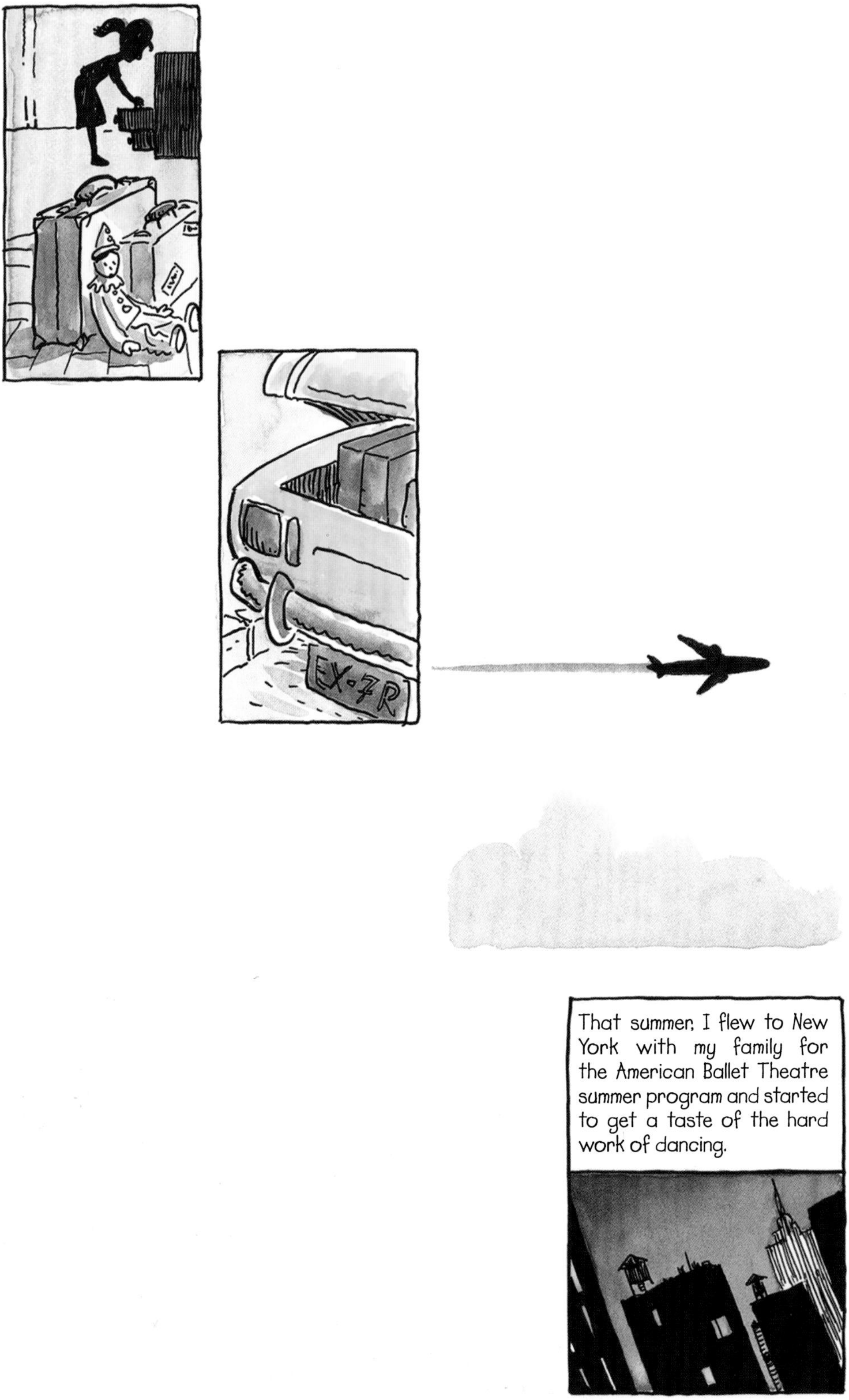
That summer, I flew to New York with my family for the American Ballet Theatre summer program and started to get a taste of the hard work of dancing.

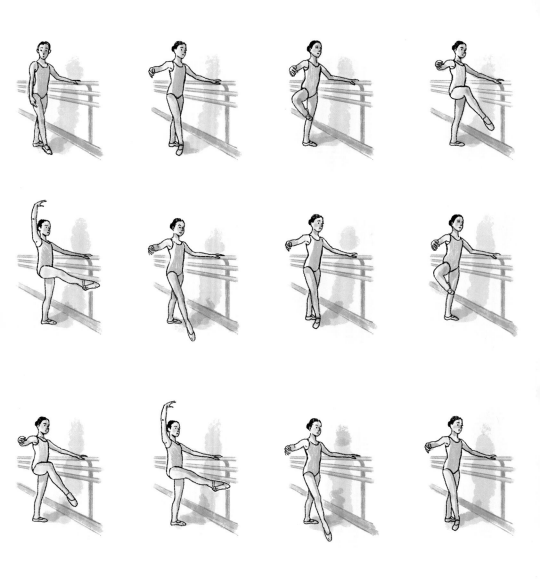

Some days I felt like I couldn't hold my legs up anymore.

A FAVORITE BOOK

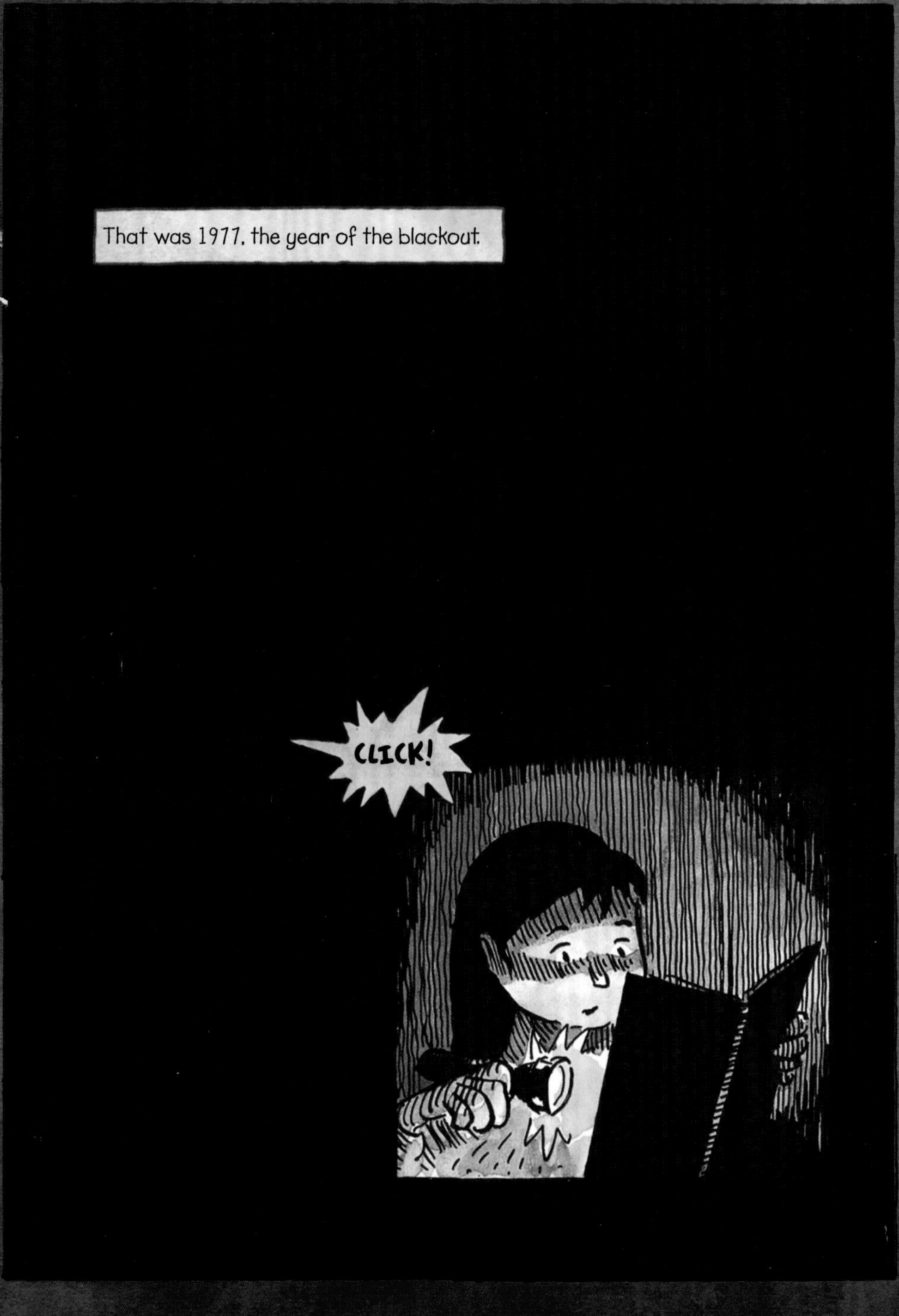
That was 1977, the year of the blackout.
CLICK!

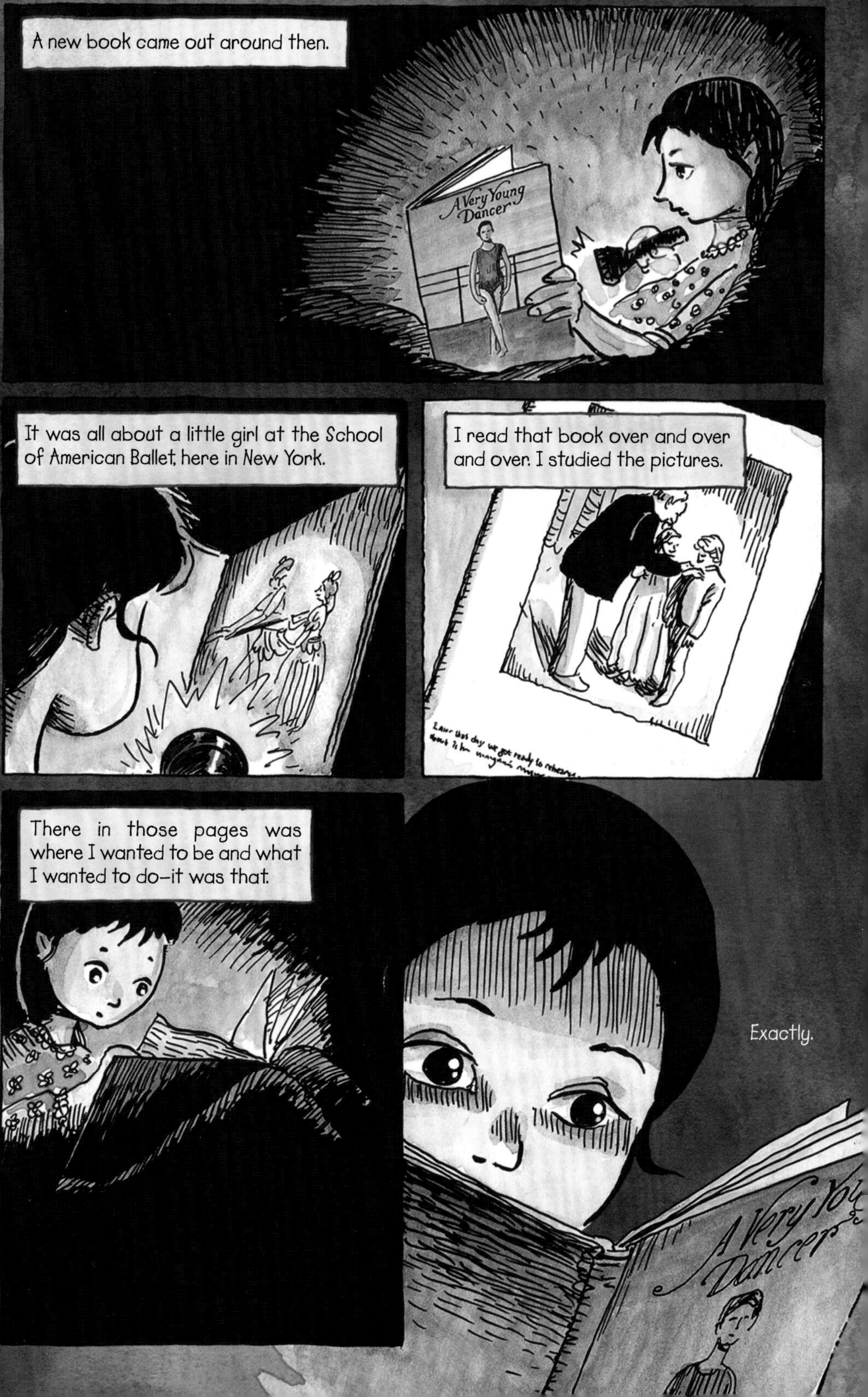
A new book came out around then.
A Very Young Dancer
It was all about a little girl at the School of American Ballet, here in New York.
I read that book over and over and over. I studied the pictures.
There in those pages was where I wanted to be and what I wanted to do—it was that.
Exactly.

BARE LEGS

A movie came out called **THE CHILDREN OF THEATRE STREET**. It was filmed at the **KIROV** school, in Leningrad.

It showed the fire of ballet being passed from one generation of dancers to another. They took dance very seriously in Russia.

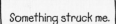

Something struck me.

The little girls in the classes, they wore leotards and ballet shoes—but they didn't wear tights.

They only started wearing them later.

These little girls all had bare legs.

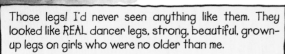

Those legs! I'd never seen anything like them. They looked like REAL dancer legs, strong, beautiful, grown-up legs on girls who were no older than me.

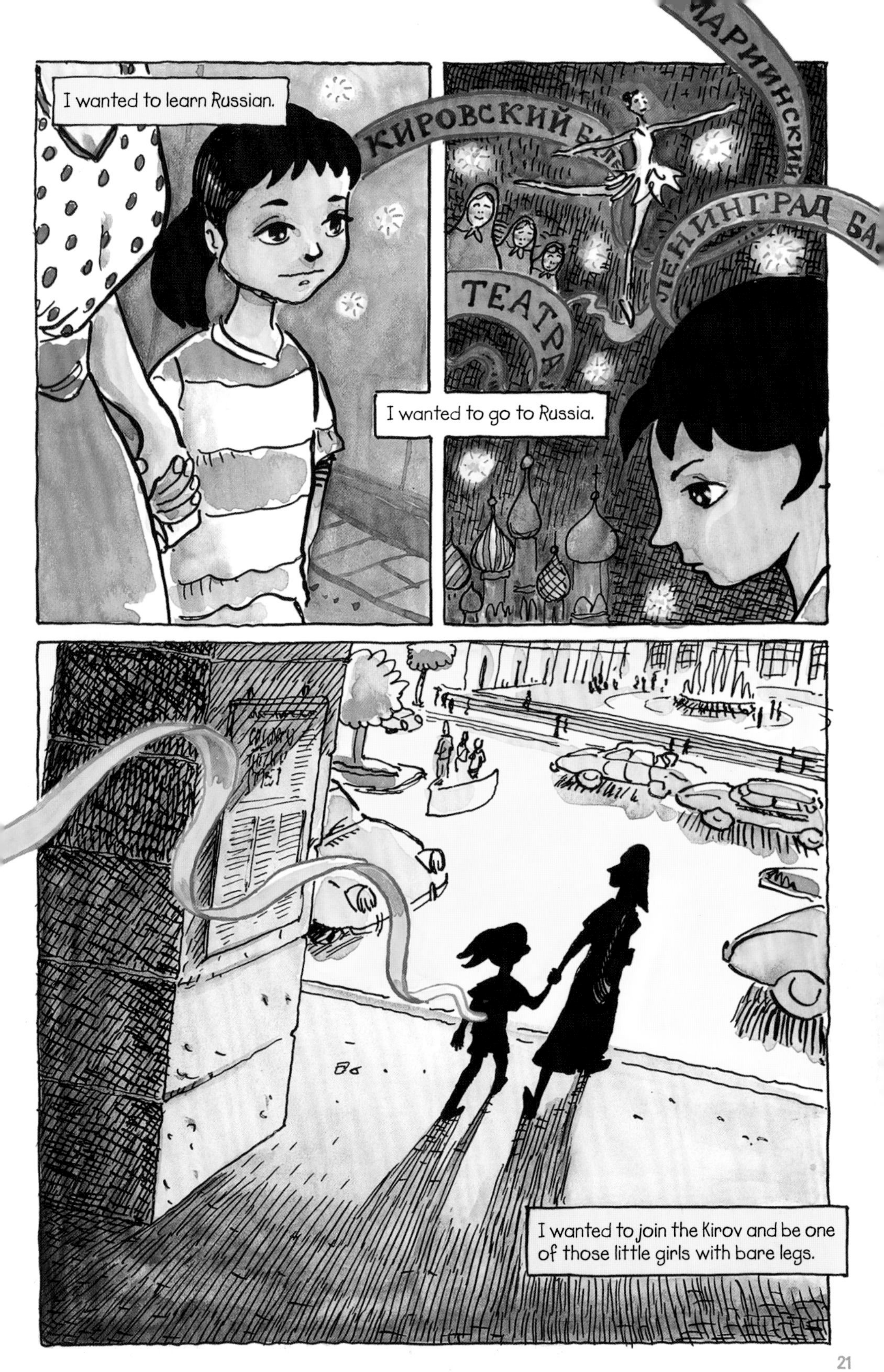
I wanted to learn Russian.
КИРОВСКИЙ
МАРИИНСКИЙ
ЛЕНИНГРАД
ТЕАТР
I wanted to go to Russia.
I wanted to join the Kirov and be one of those little girls with bare legs.

audition

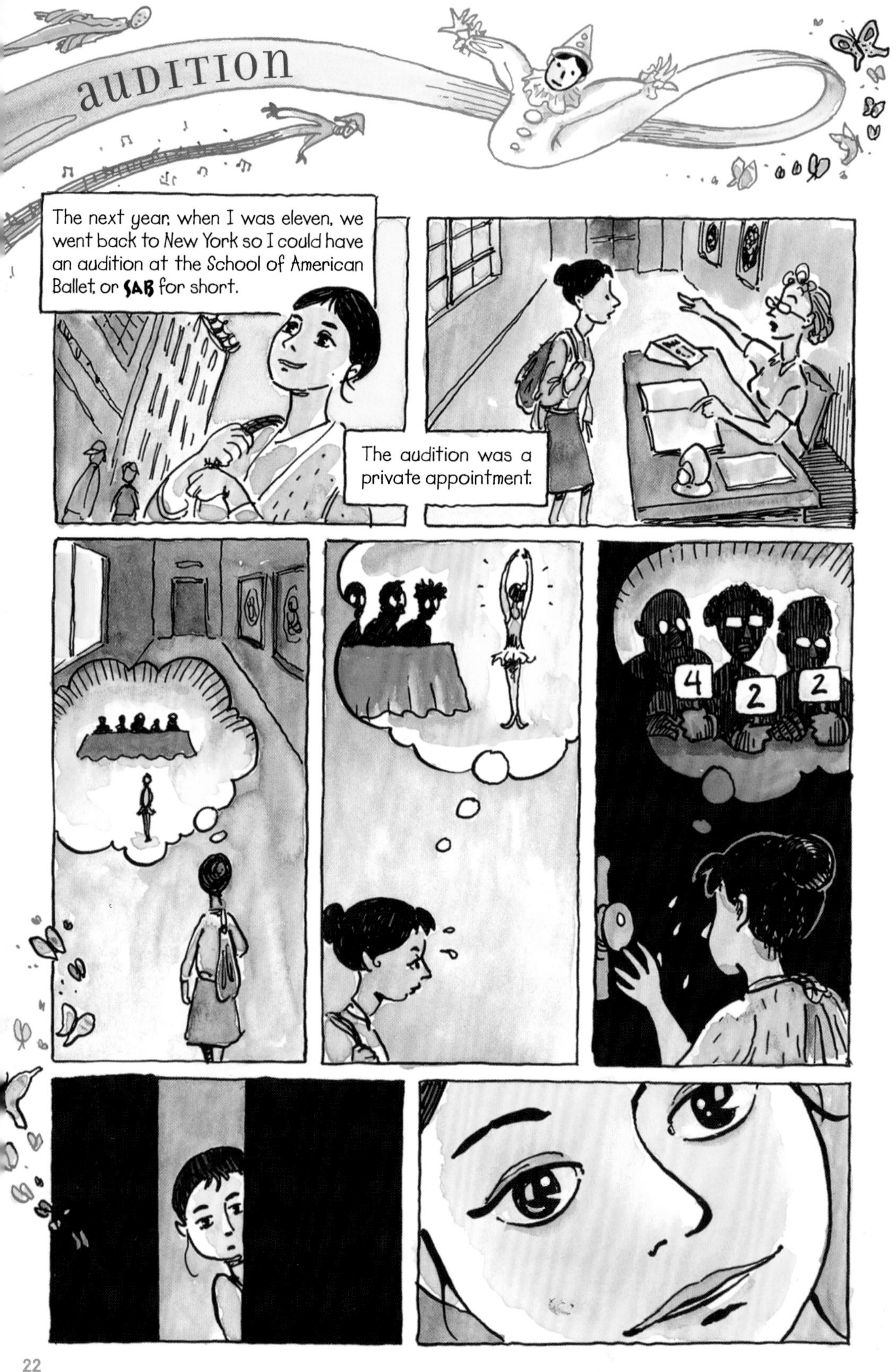
The next year, when I was eleven, we went back to New York so I could have an audition at the School of American Ballet, or SAB for short.
The audition was a private appointment.
4
2
2

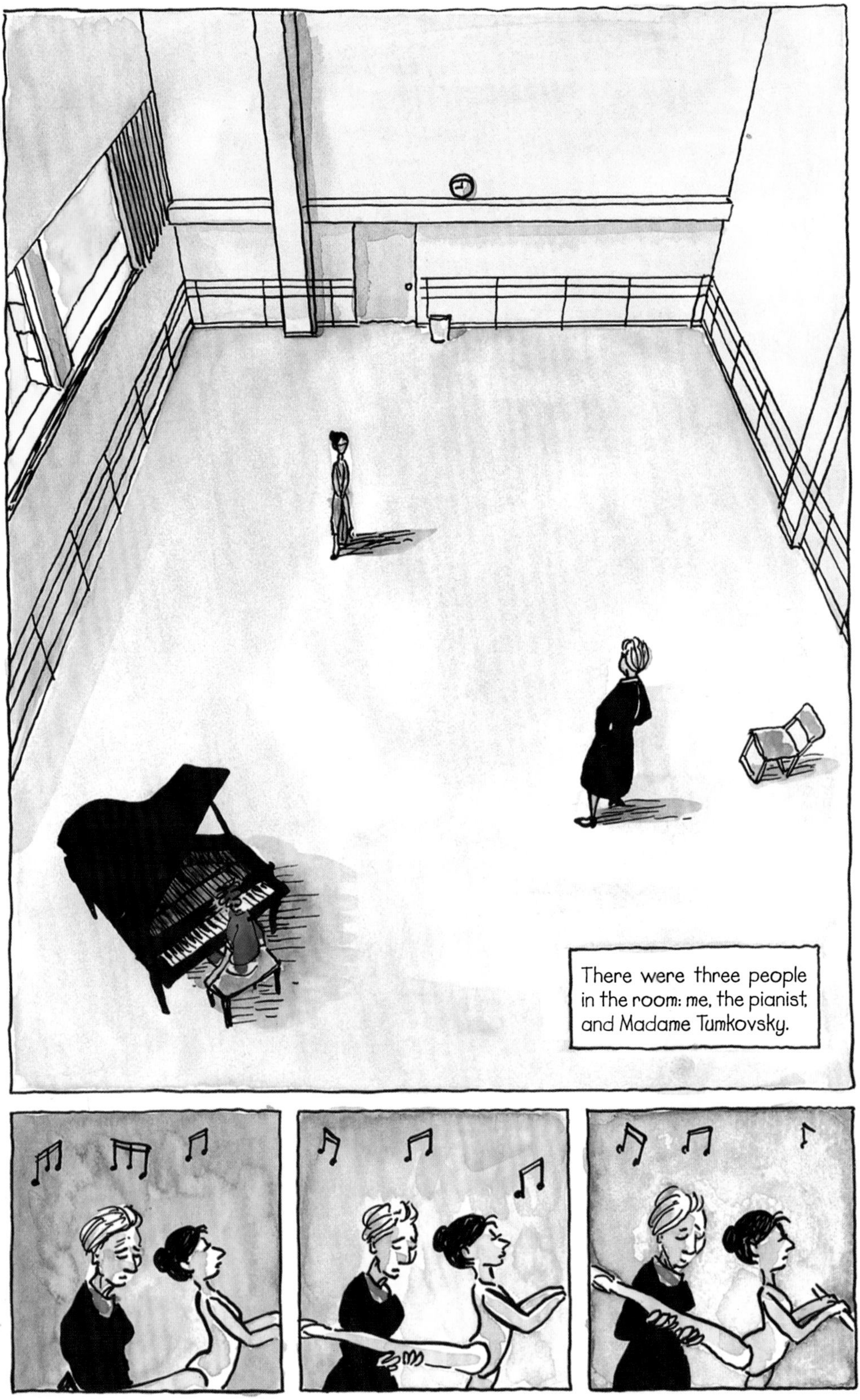
There were three people in the room: me, the pianist, and Madame Tumkovsky.

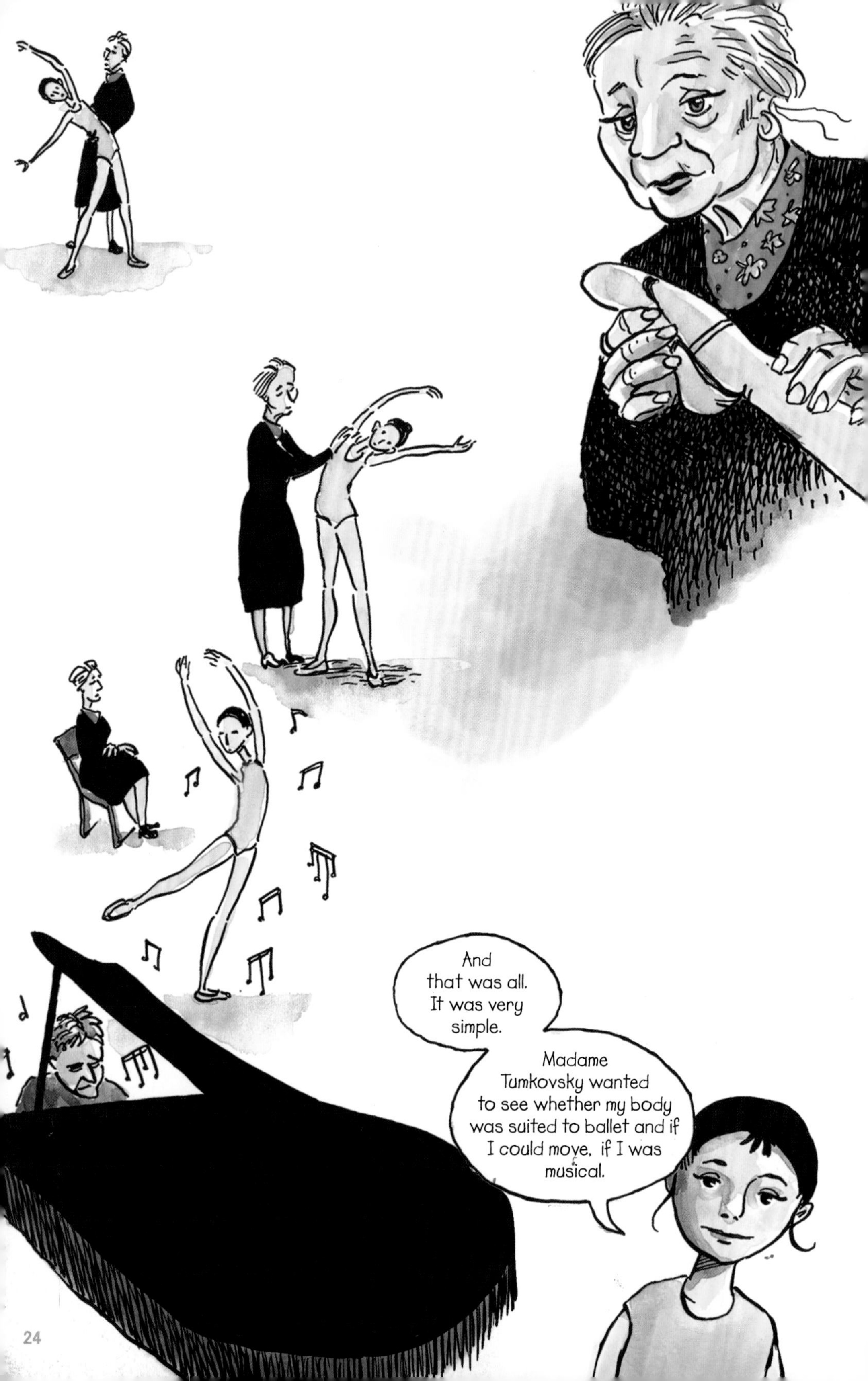

And that was all. It was very simple.
Madame Tumkovsky wanted to see whether my body was suited to ballet and if I could move, if I was musical.

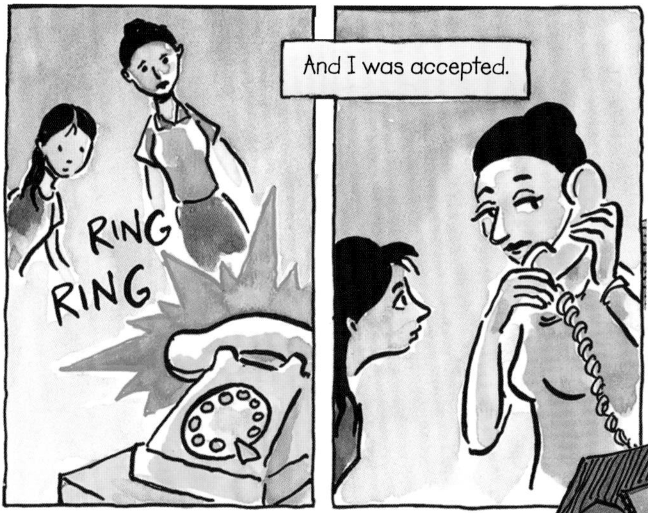
RING
RING
And I was accepted.

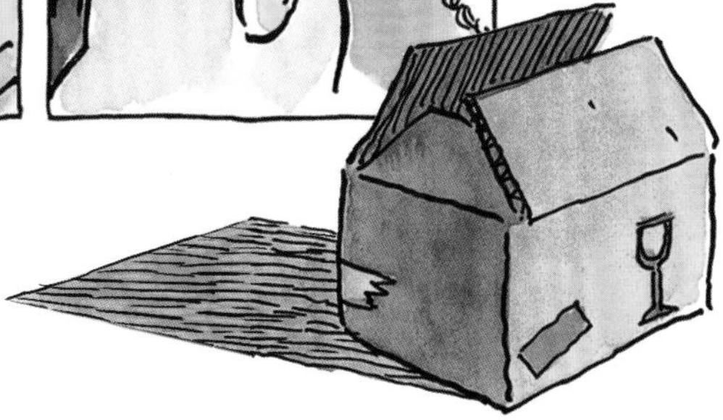

My family decided to move to New York for good, so I could go to the school.

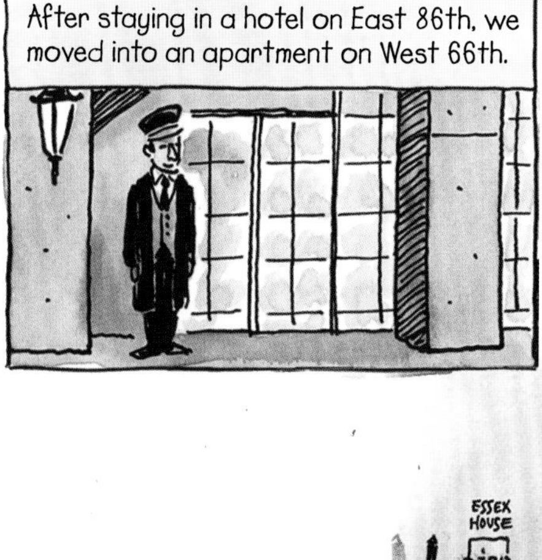
After staying in a hotel on East 86th, we moved into an apartment on West 66th.

I didn't see Daddy very much anymore.
He was back in San Juan a lot.
At the time, I thought it
was for his work.

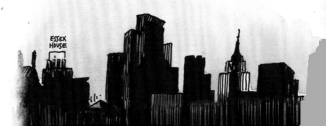

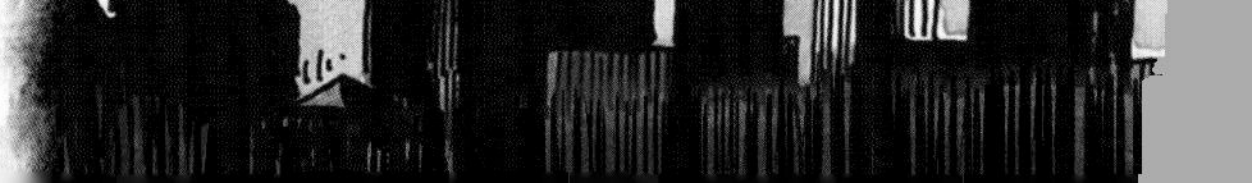
ESSEX
HOUSE

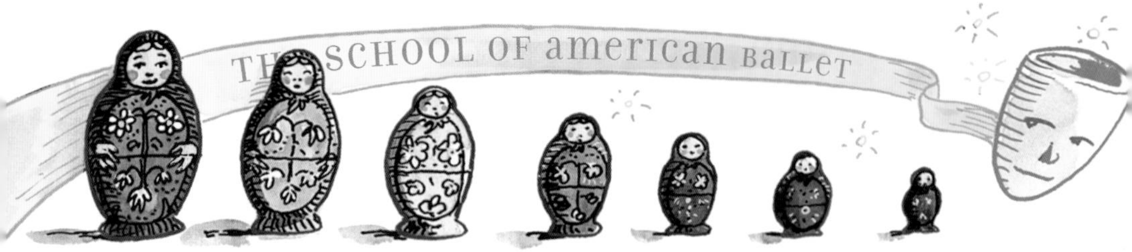

THE SCHOOL OF AMERICAN BALLET

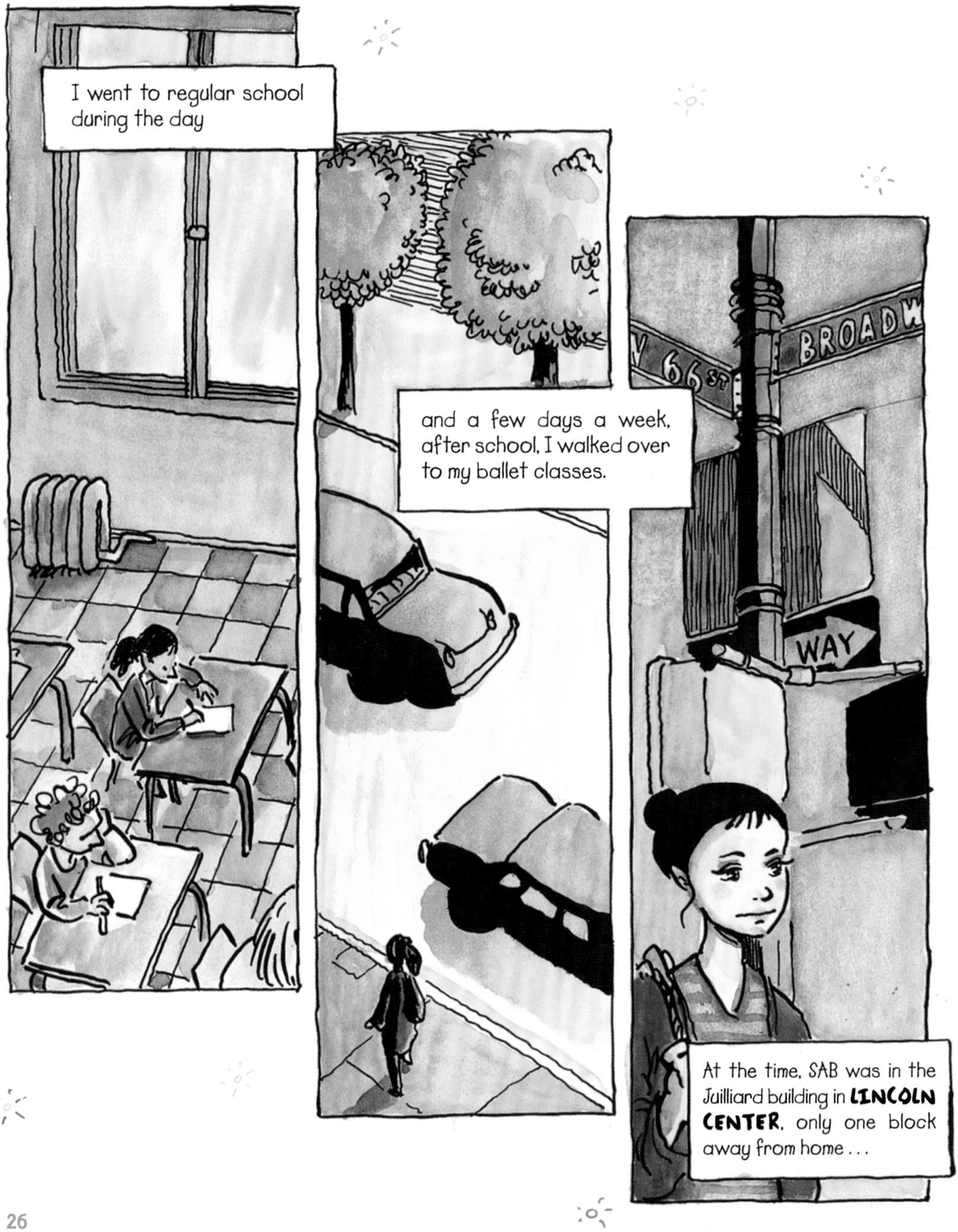

I went to regular school during the day
and a few days a week, after school, I walked over to my ballet classes.
W 66 ST
BROADW
WAY
At the time, SAB was in the Juilliard building in **LINCOLN CENTER**, only one block away from home . . .

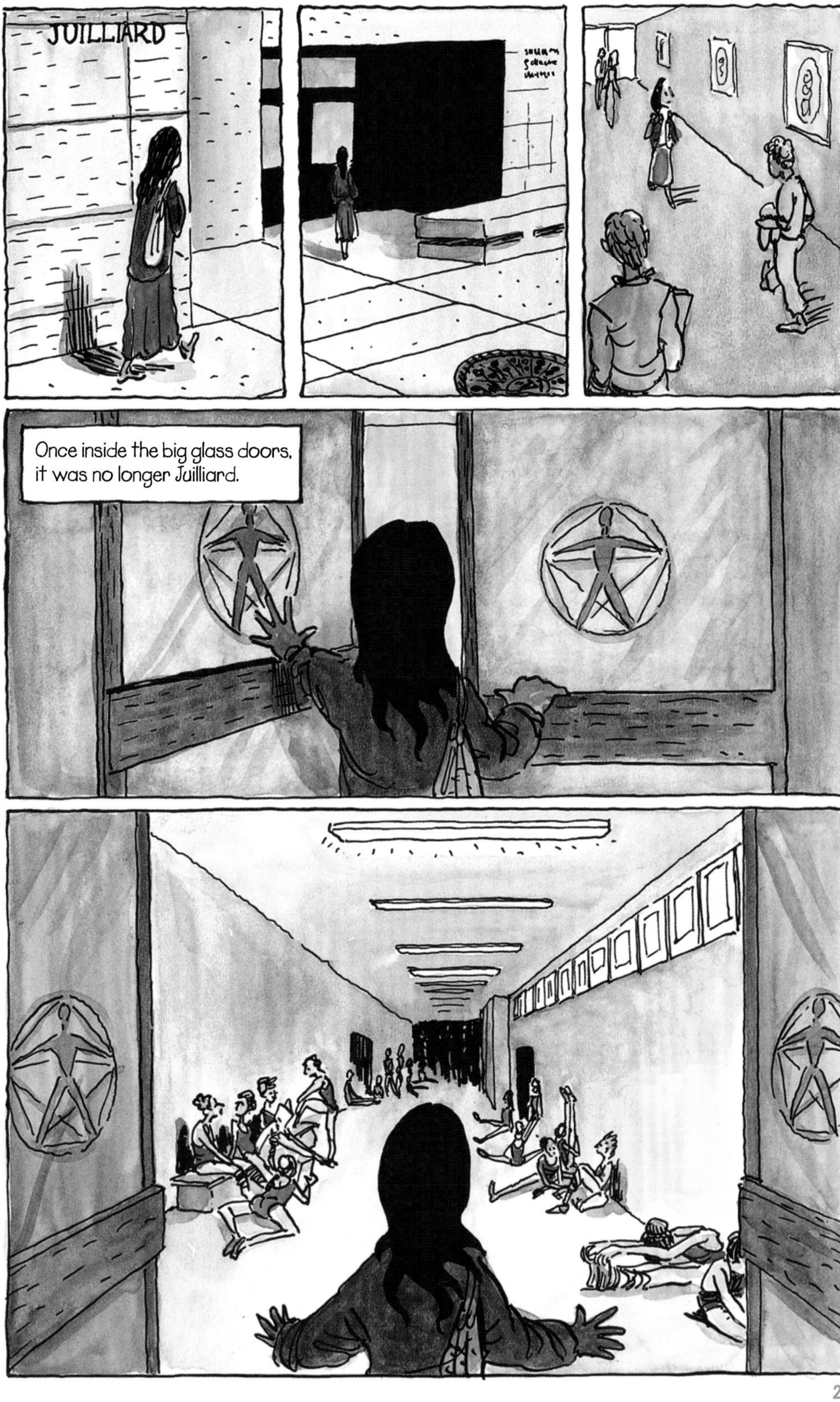
JUILLIARD
Once inside the big glass doors, it was no longer Juilliard.

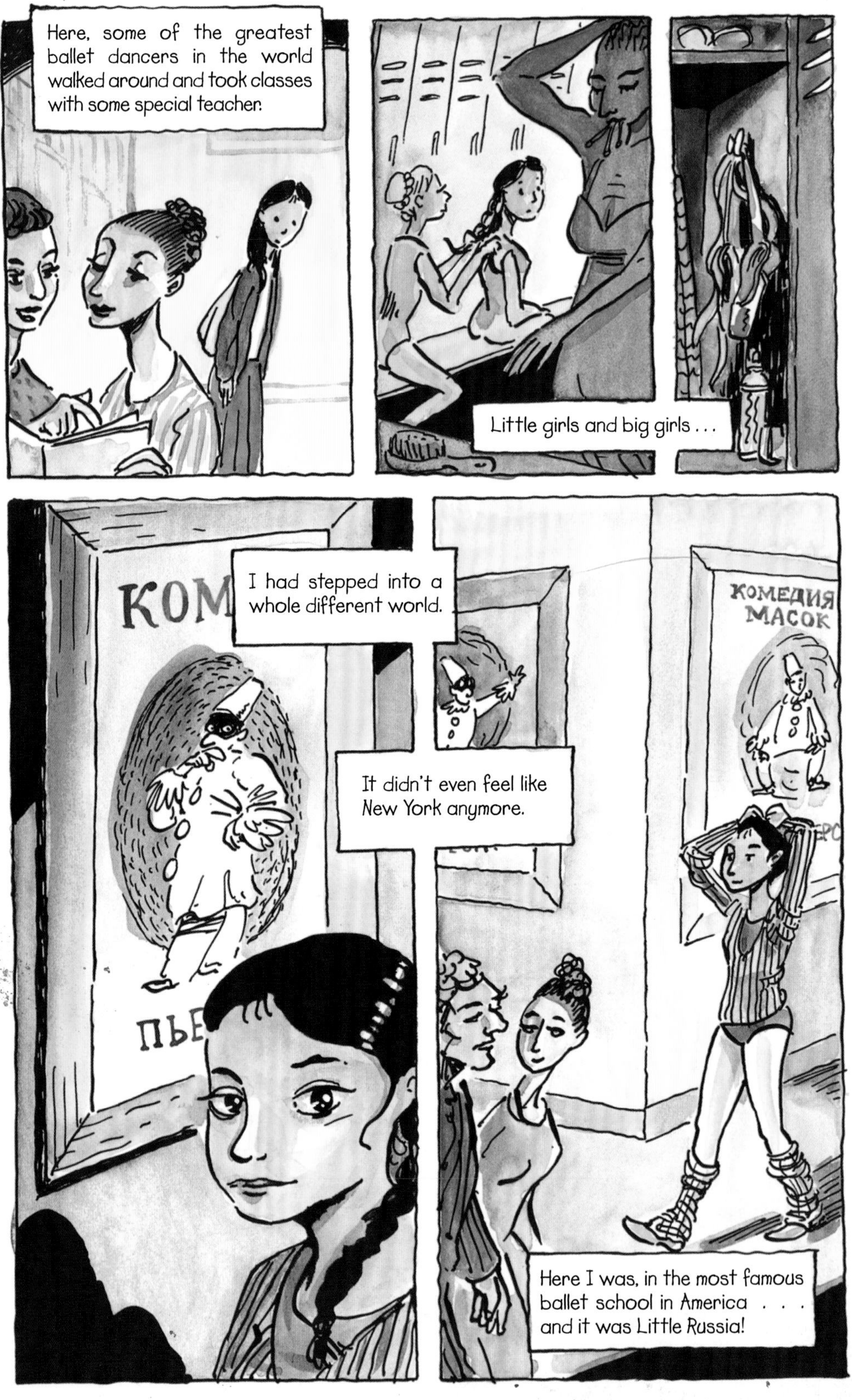

Here, some of the greatest ballet dancers in the world walked around and took classes with some special teacher.
Little girls and big girls . . .
КОМ
ПЬЕ
I had stepped into a whole different world.
It didn't even feel like New York anymore.
КОМЕДИЯ МАСОК
Here I was, in the most famous ballet school in America . . . and it was Little Russia!

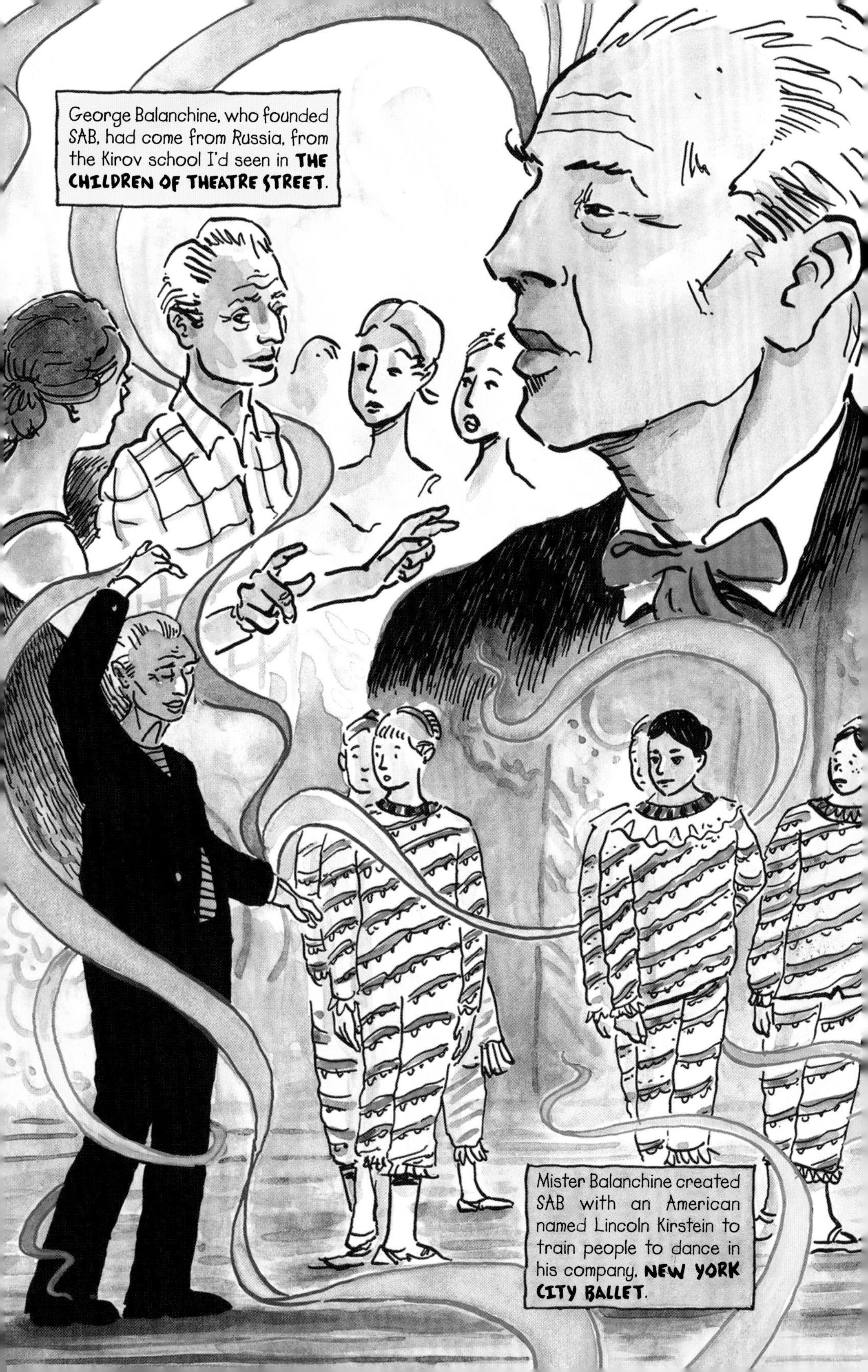
George Balanchine, who founded SAB, had come from Russia, from the Kirov school I'd seen in **THE CHILDREN OF THEATRE STREET**.
Mister Balanchine created SAB with an American named Lincoln Kirstein to train people to dance in his company, **NEW YORK CITY BALLET**.

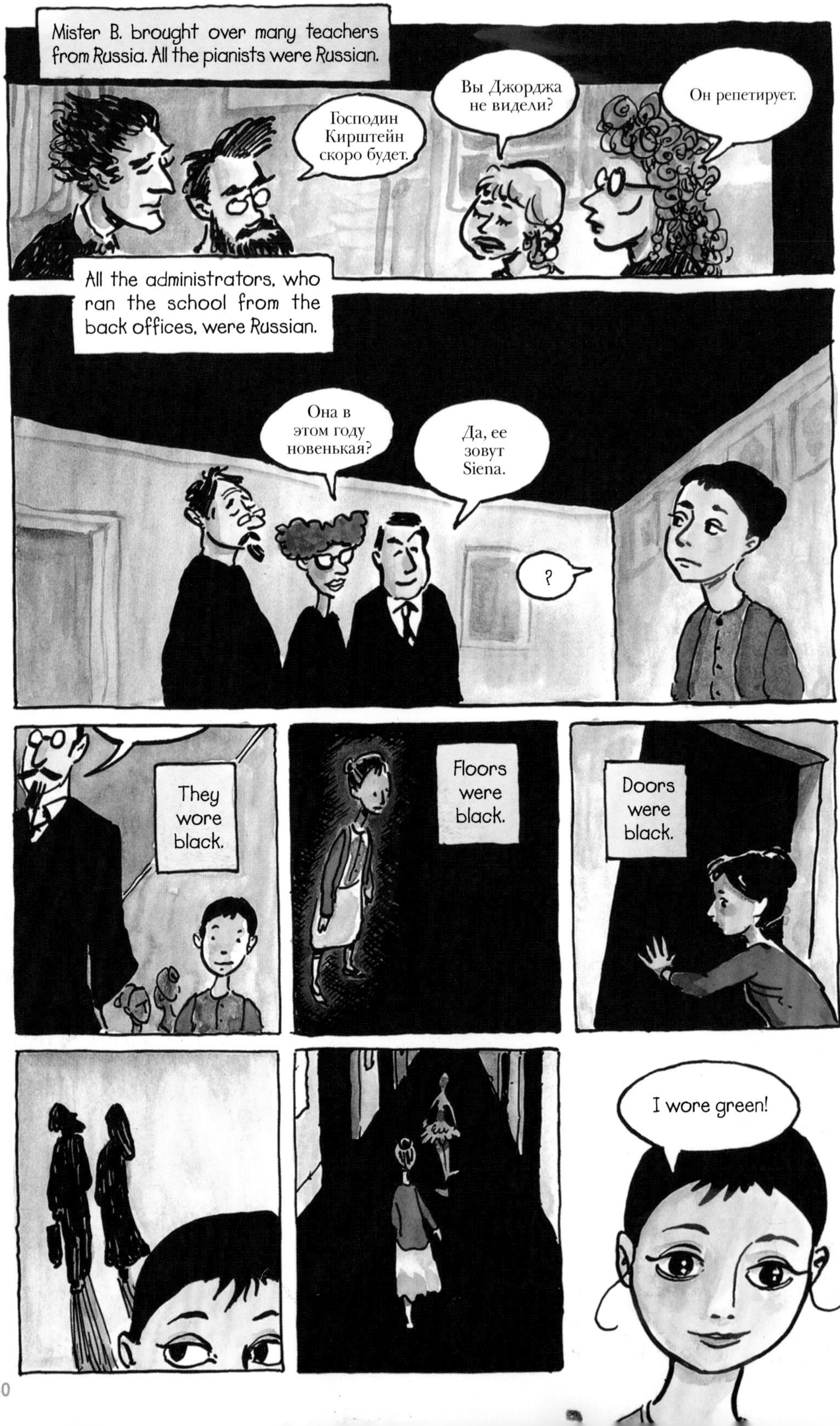

Mister B. brought over many teachers from Russia. All the pianists were Russian.
Господин Кирштейн скоро будет.
Вы Джорджа не видели?
Он репетирует.
All the administrators, who ran the school from the back offices, were Russian.
Она в этом году новенькая?
Да, ее зовут Siena.
?
They wore black.
Floors were black.
Doors were black.
I wore green!

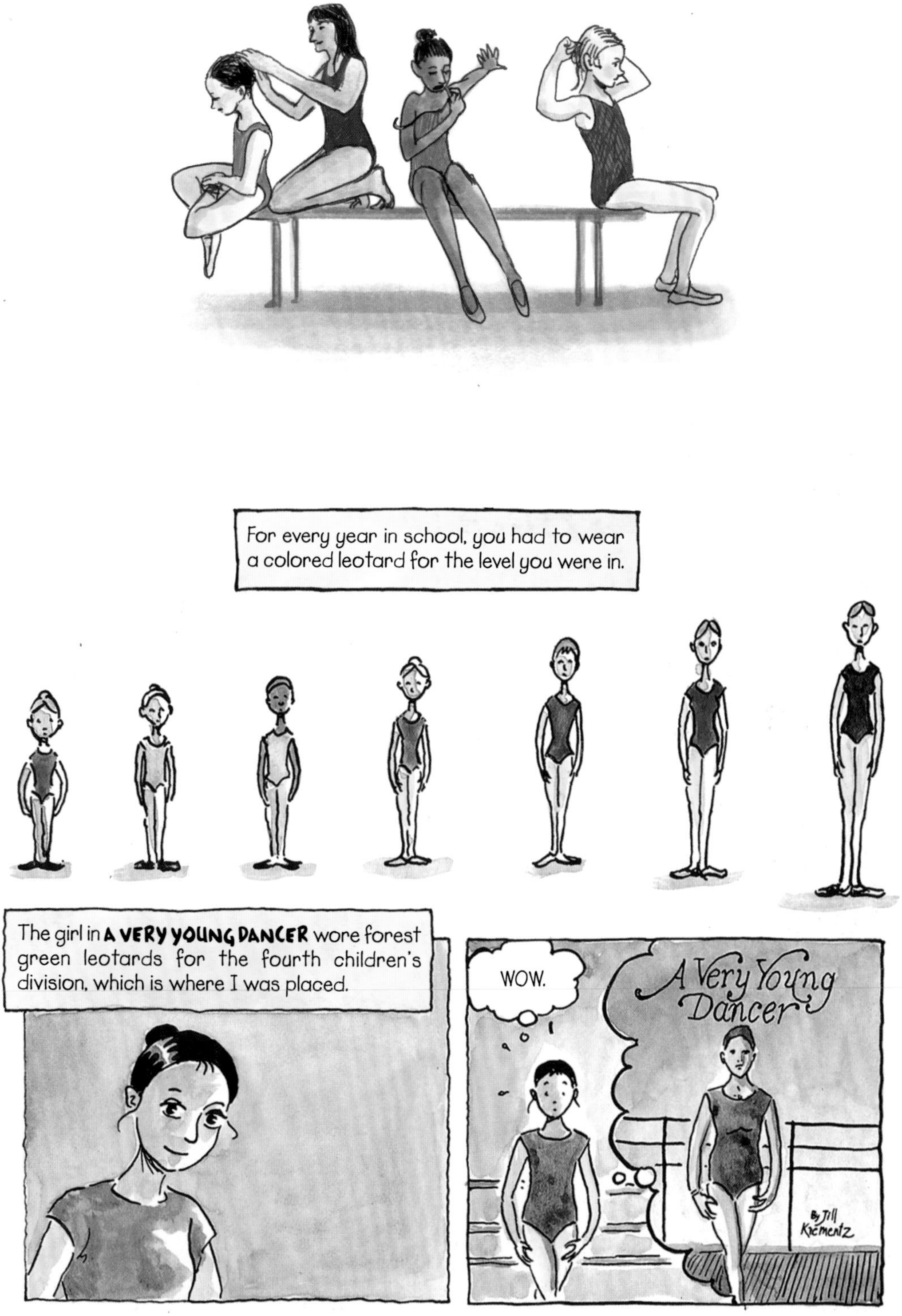
For every year in school, you had to wear a colored leotard for the level you were in.
The girl in A VERY YOUNG DANCER wore forest green leotards for the fourth children's division, which is where I was placed.
WOW.
A Very Young Dancer
By Jill Krementz

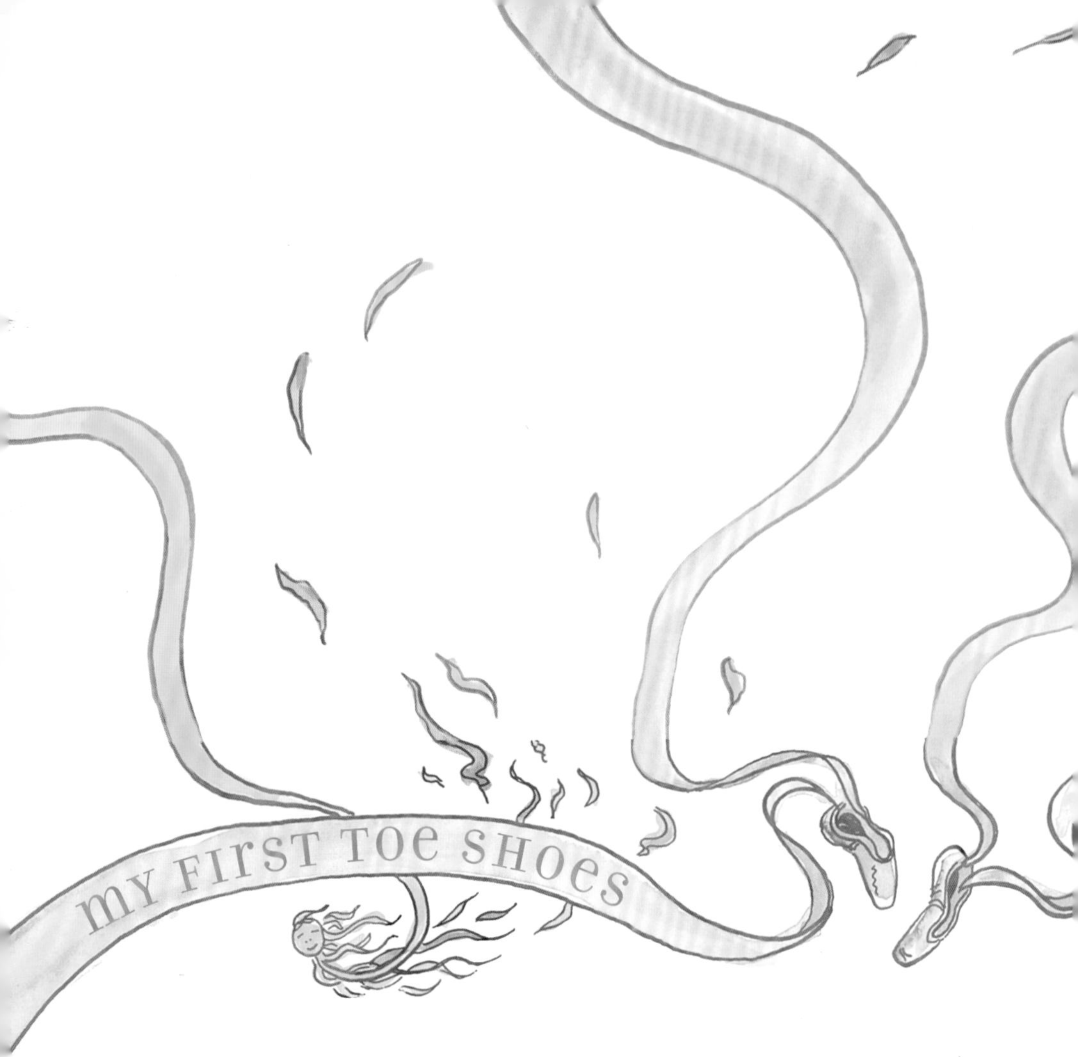
MY FIRST TOE SHOES

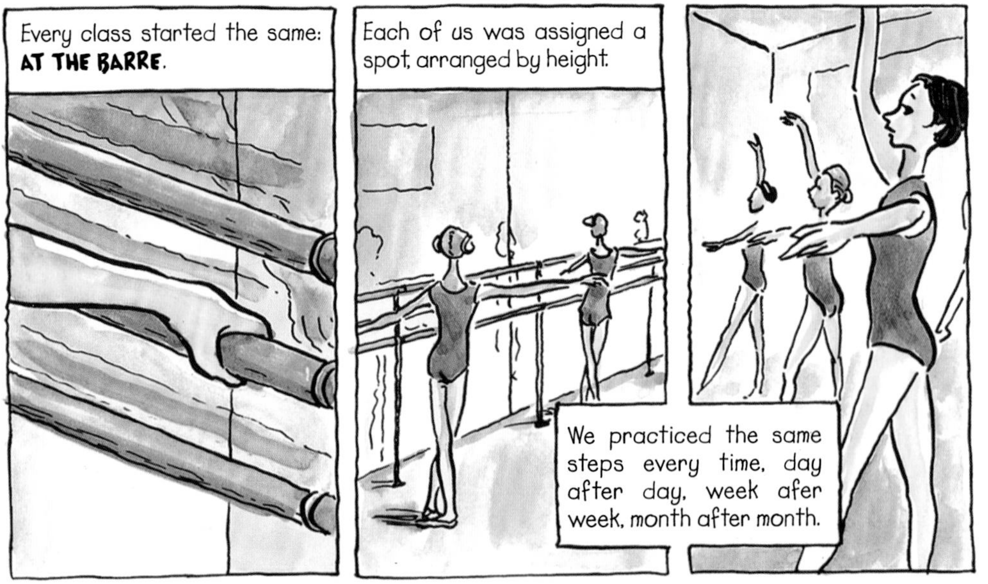
Every class started the same: **AT THE BARRE**.
Each of us was assigned a spot, arranged by height.
We practiced the same steps every time, day after day, week afer week, month after month.

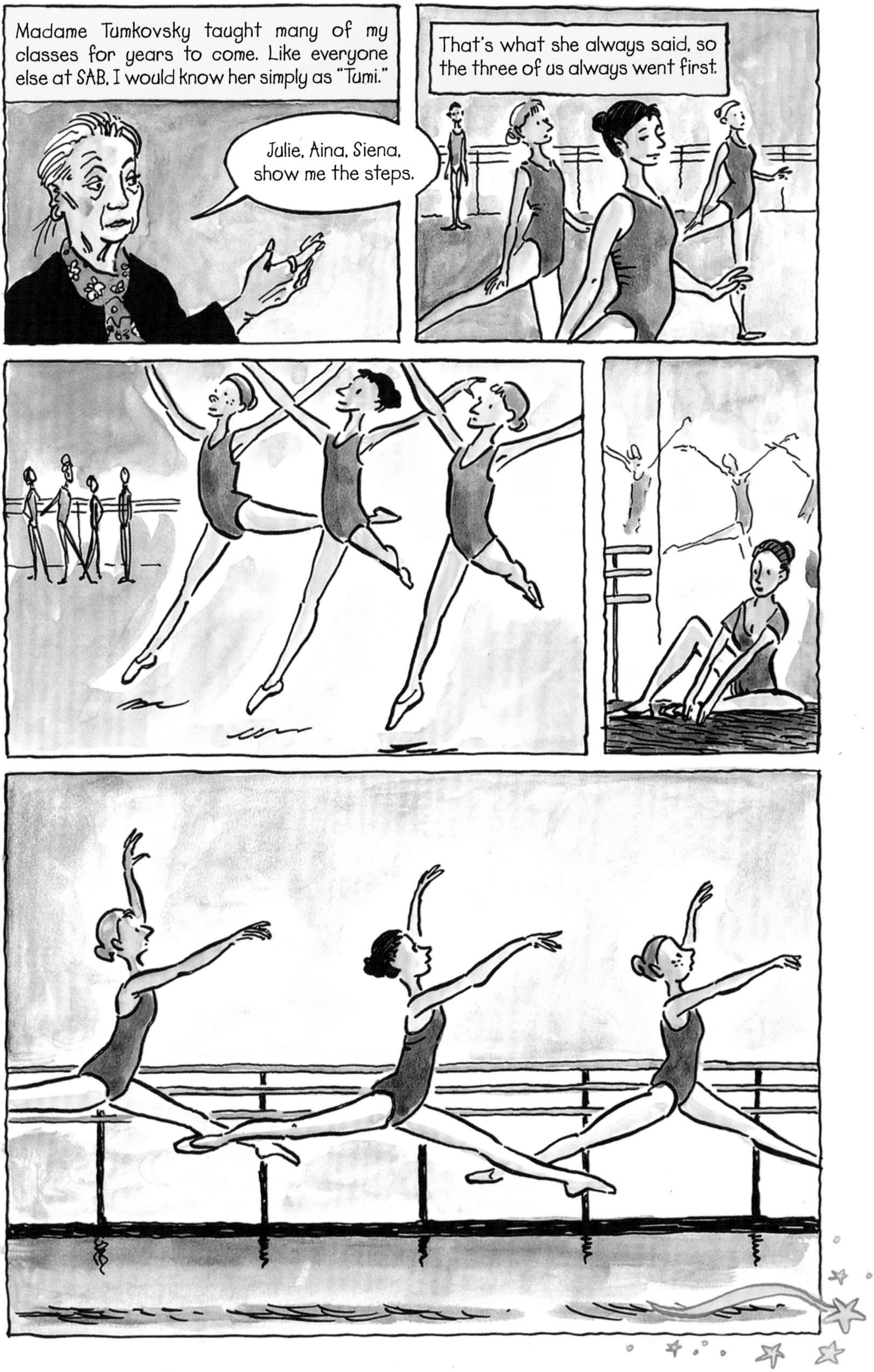
Madame Tumkovsky taught many of my classes for years to come. Like everyone else at SAB, I would know her simply as "Tumi."
Julie, Aina, Siena, show me the steps.
That's what she always said, so the three of us always went first.

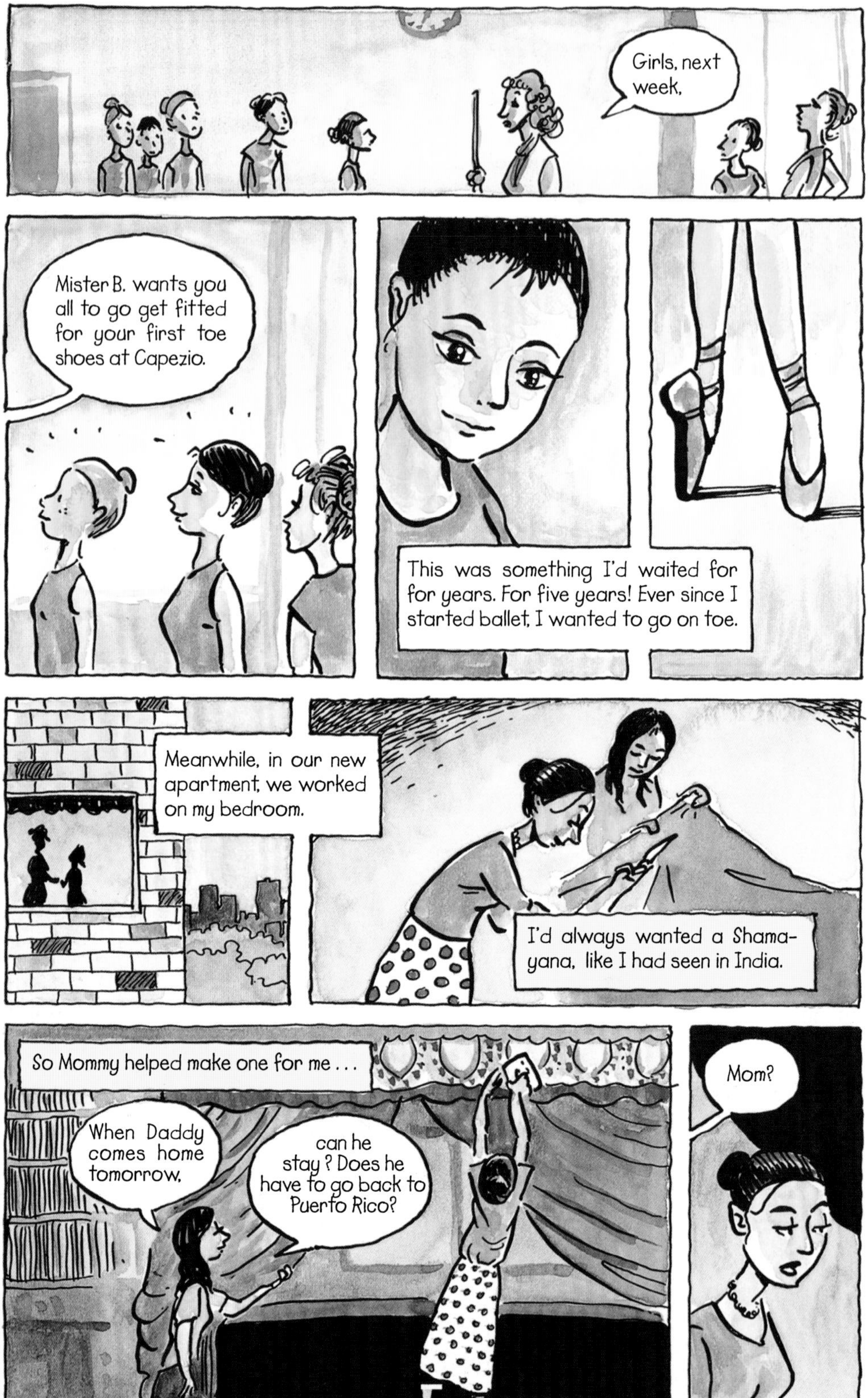
Girls, next week,
Mister B. wants you all to go get fitted for your first toe shoes at Capezio.
This was something I'd waited for for years. For five years! Ever since I started ballet, I wanted to go on toe.
Meanwhile, in our new apartment, we worked on my bedroom.
I'd always wanted a Shama-yana, like I had seen in India.
So Mommy helped make one for me . . .
When Daddy comes home tomorrow,
can he stay ? Does he have to go back to Puerto Rico?
Mom?

Daddy arrived the next afternoon. He could only stay for two weeks.

Sienita!

How would you like your own barre?

He made the other half of my bedroom into a ballet studio with my own little barre and mirror.

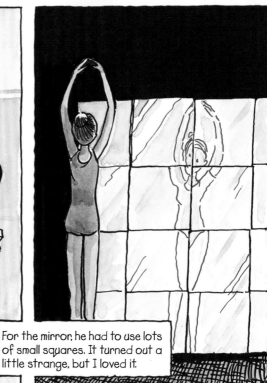

For the mirror, he had to use lots of small squares. It turned out a little strange, but I loved it.

At Capezio's, someone named Judy Weiss made sure we got exactly the right fit for our first toe shoes.

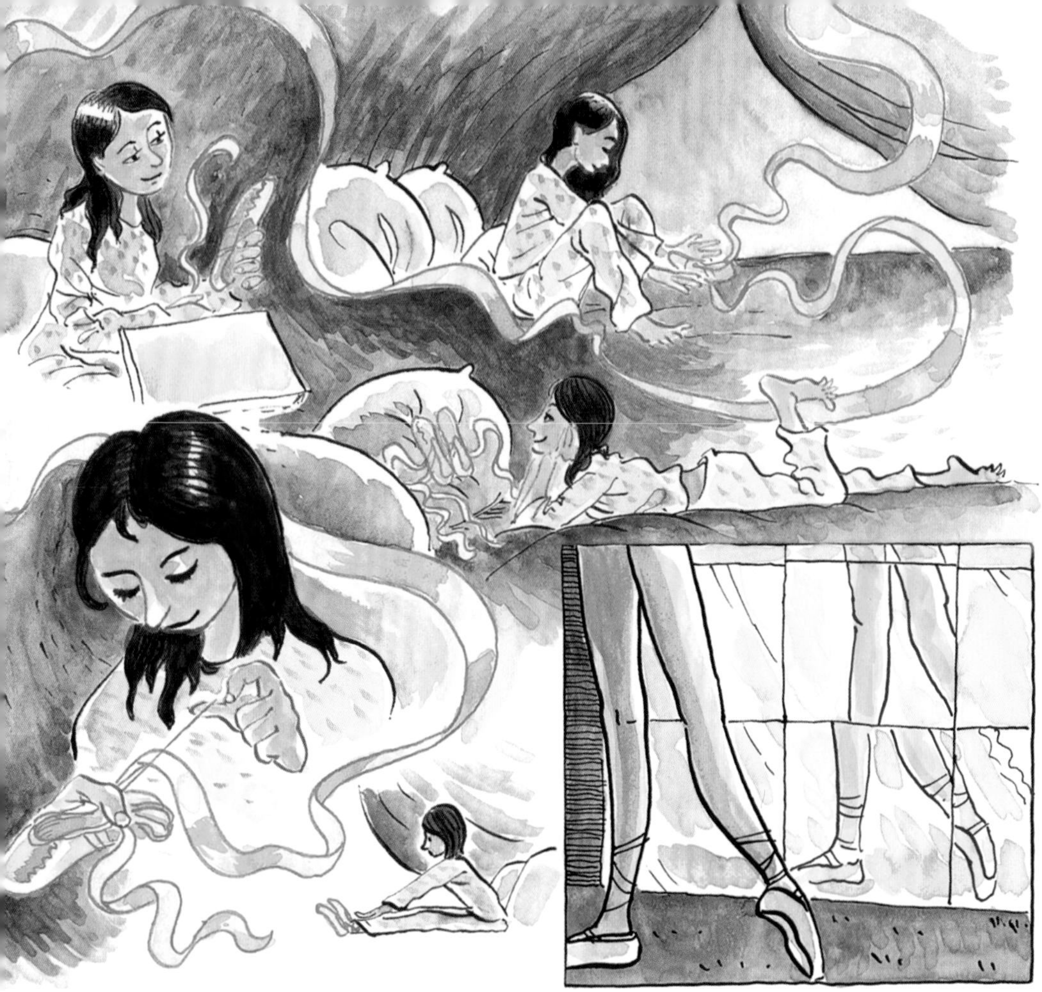

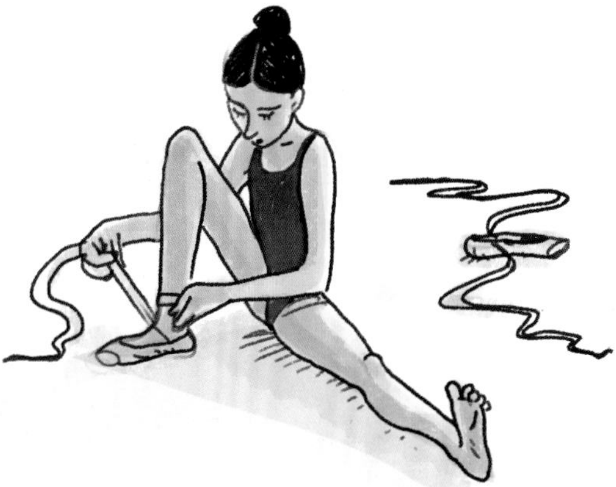

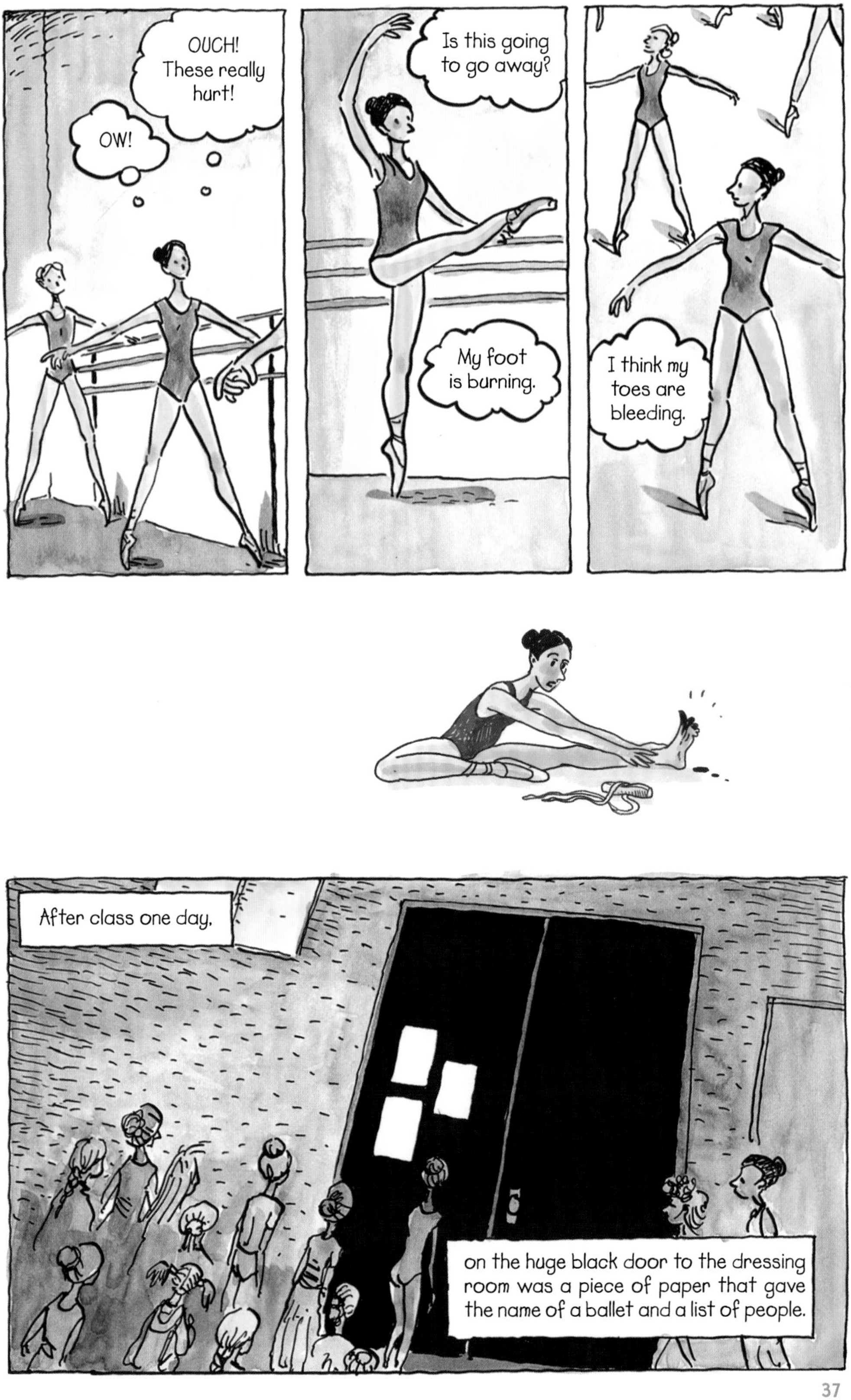
OUCH! These really hurt!
OW!
Is this going to go away?
My foot is burning.
I think my toes are bleeding.
After class one day,
on the huge black door to the dressing room was a piece of paper that gave the name of a ballet and a list of people.

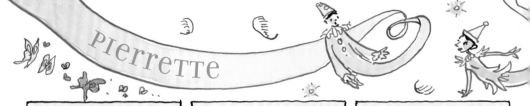

Mister Balanchine choreographed many ballets with parts for children.

That day we found out who had been cast in this ballet.

And all the children were from the school.

I looked down the list, and there was my name!

Not everyone was selected.

We began to have rehearsals on top of classes, for one ballet after another:

COPPELIA...

THE NUTCRACKER...

A MIDSUMMER NIGHT'S DREAM.

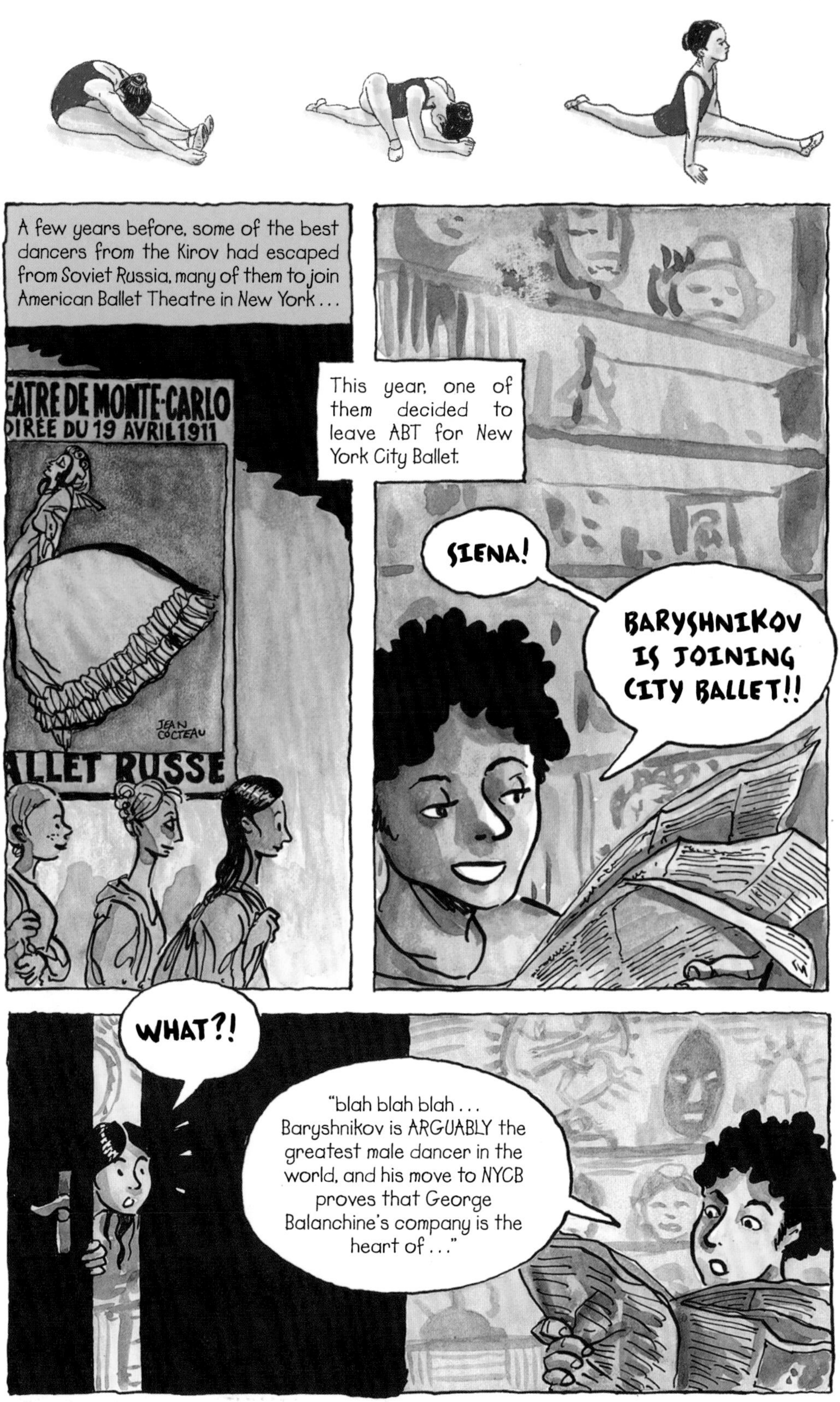
A few years before, some of the best dancers from the Kirov had escaped from Soviet Russia, many of them to join American Ballet Theatre in New York . . .
EATRE DE MONTE-CARLO
DIRÉE DU 19 AVRIL 1911
JEAN COCTEAU
ALLET RUSSE
This year, one of them decided to leave ABT for New York City Ballet.
SIENA!
BARYSHNIKOV IS JOINING CITY BALLET!!
WHAT?!
"blah blah blah . . . Baryshnikov is ARGUABLY the greatest male dancer in the world, and his move to NYCB proves that George Balanchine's company is the heart of . . ."

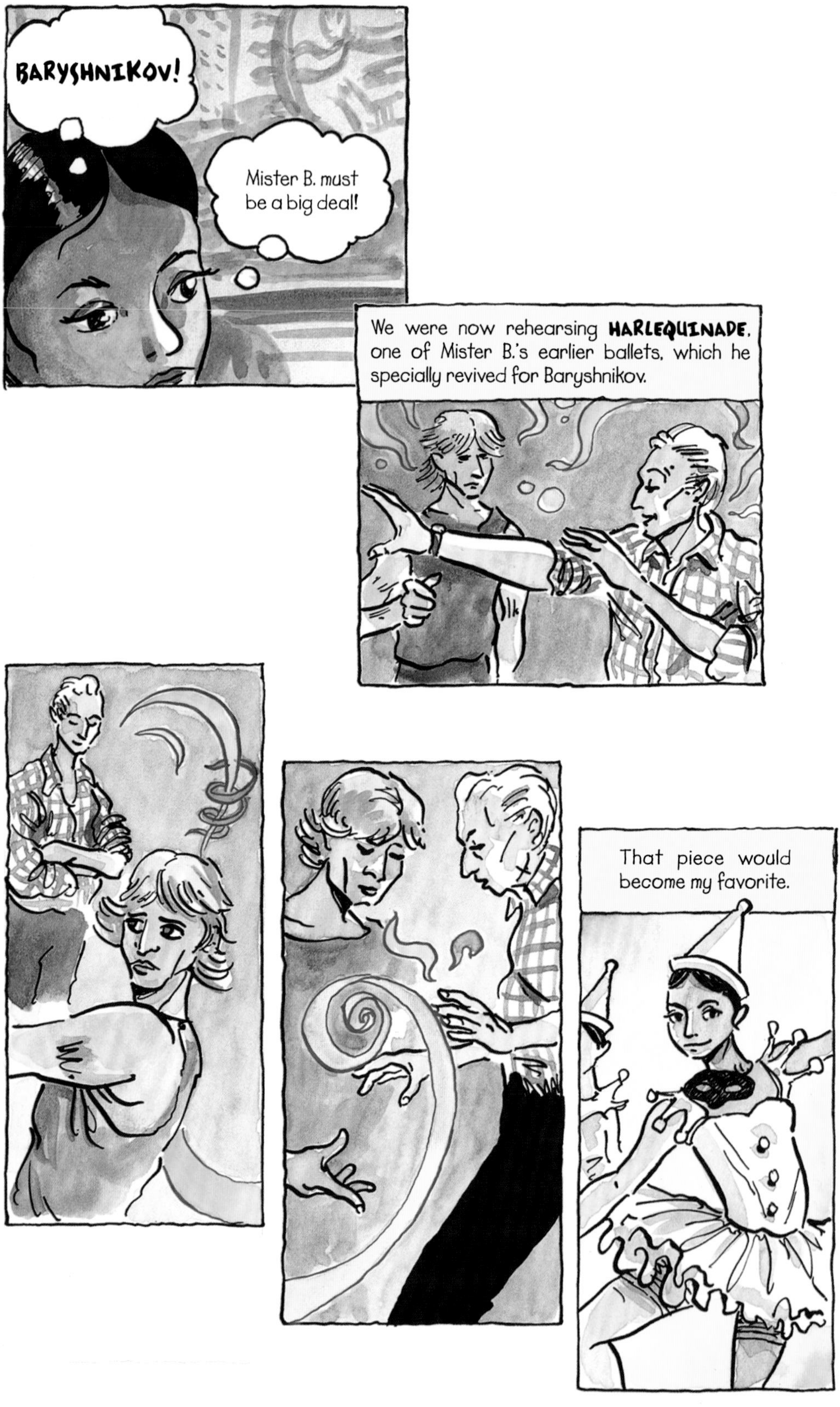
BARYSHNIKOV!
Mister B. must be a big deal!
We were now rehearsing HARLEQUINADE, one of Mister B.'s earlier ballets, which he specially revived for Baryshnikov.
That piece would become my favorite.

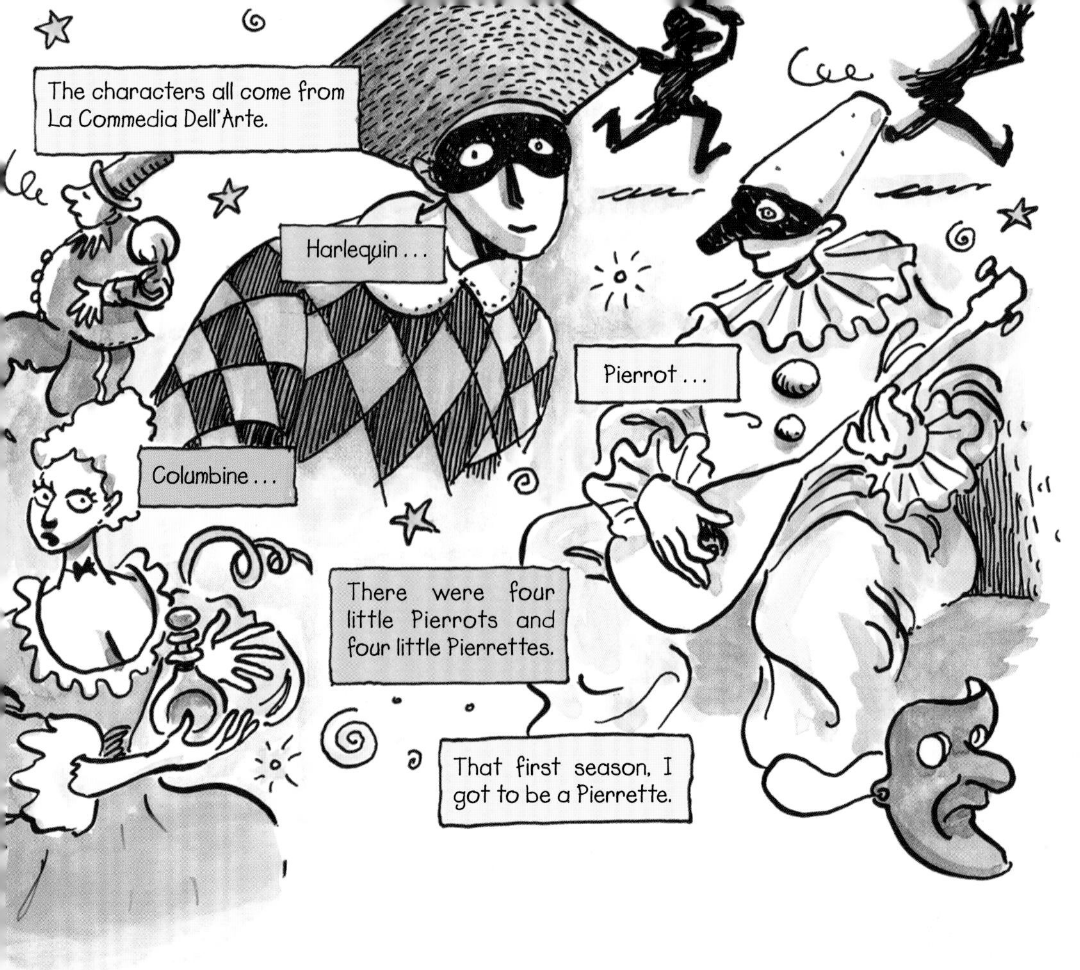
The characters all come from La Commedia Dell'Arte.
Harlequin . . .
Pierrot . . .
Columbine . . .
There were four little Pierrots and four little Pierrettes.
That first season, I got to be a Pierrette.

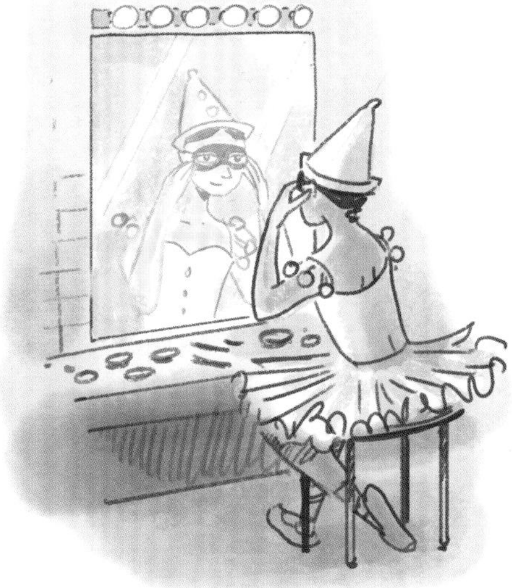

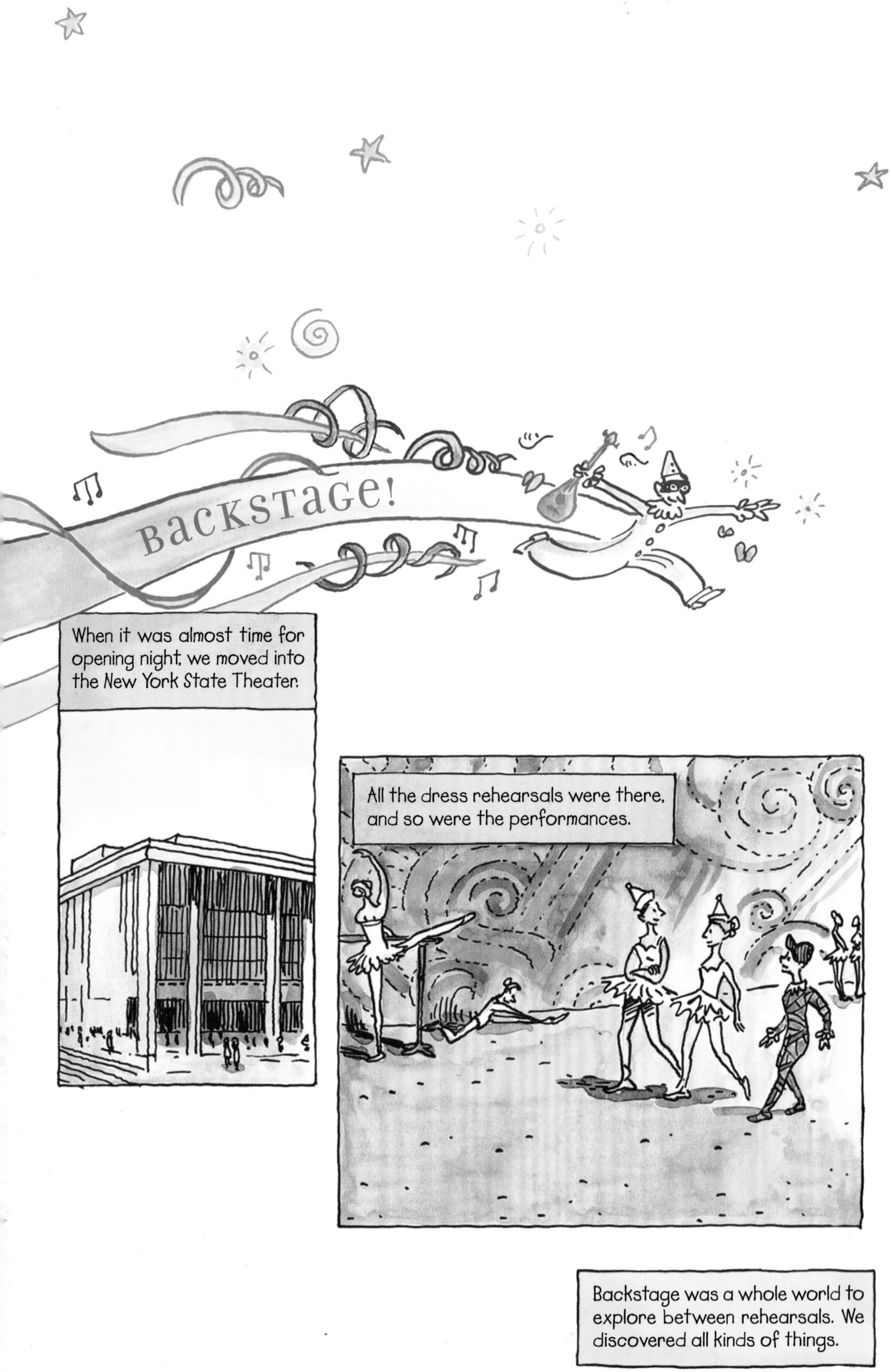
BACKSTAGE!
When it was almost time for opening night, we moved into the New York State Theater.
All the dress rehearsals were there, and so were the performances.
Backstage was a whole world to explore between rehearsals. We discovered all kinds of things.

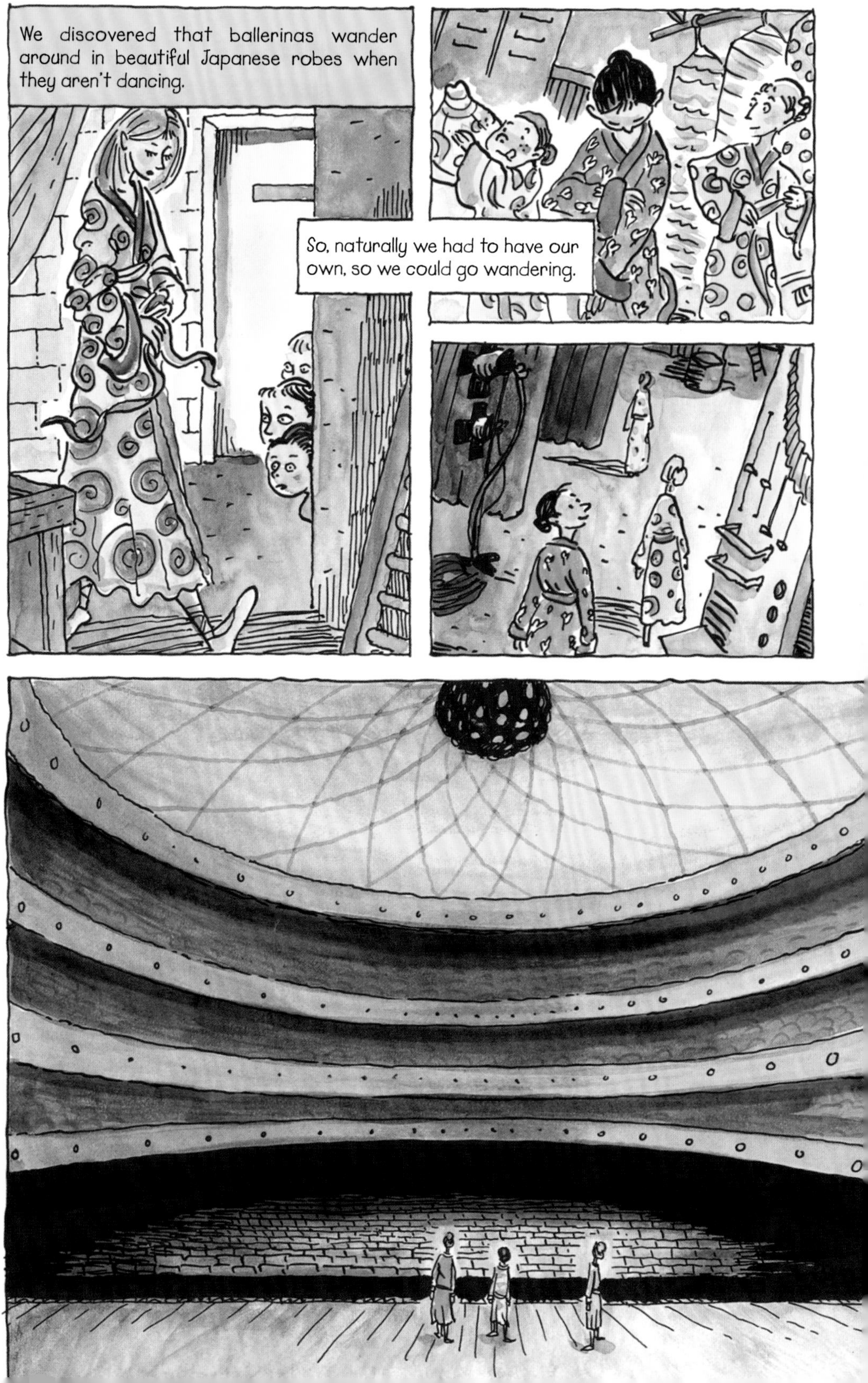
We discovered that ballerinas wander around in beautiful Japanese robes when they aren't dancing.
So, naturally we had to have our own, so we could go wandering.

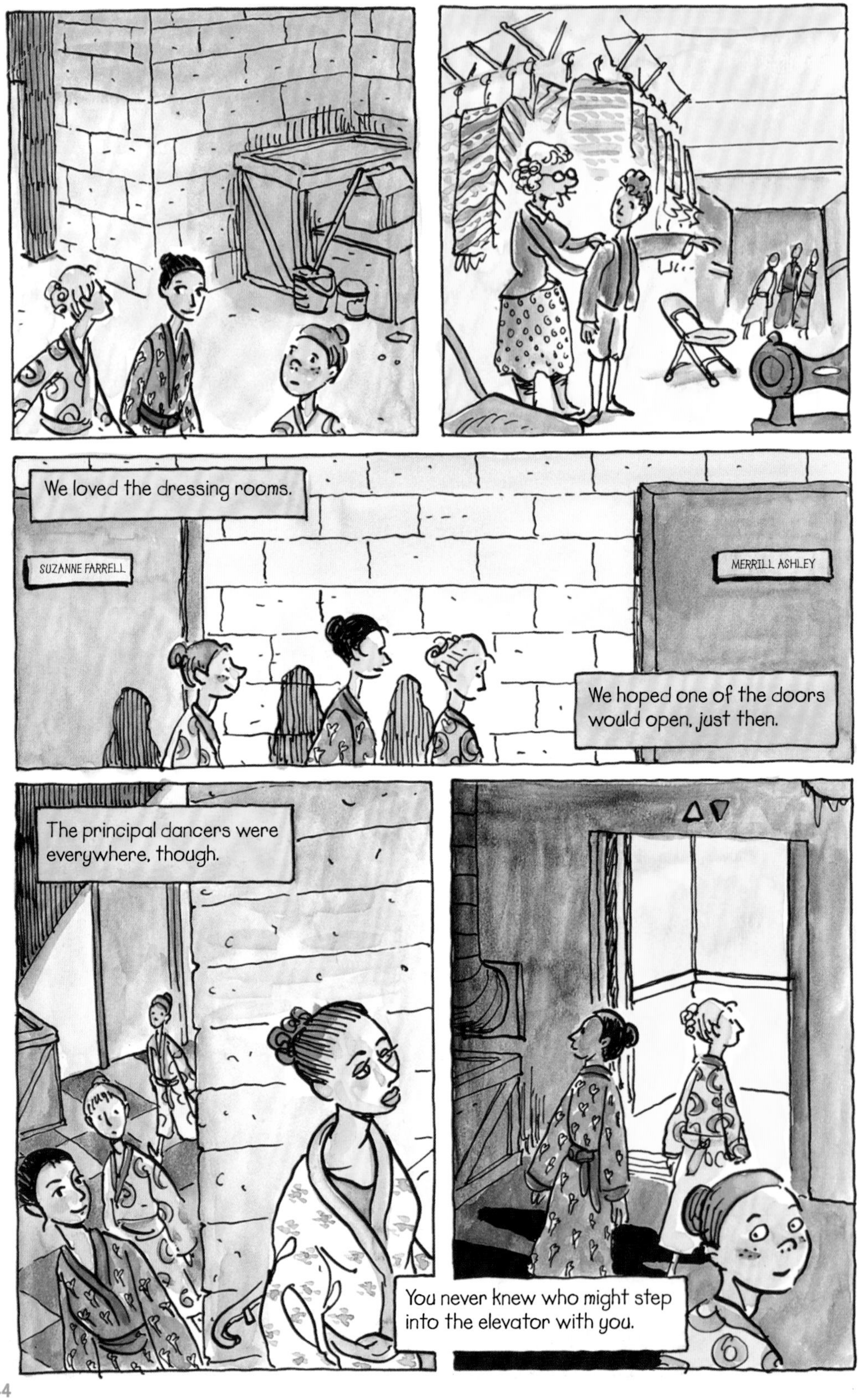
We loved the dressing rooms.
SUZANNE FARRELL
MERRILL ASHLEY
We hoped one of the doors would open, just then.
The principal dancers were everywhere, though.
You never knew who might step into the elevator with you.

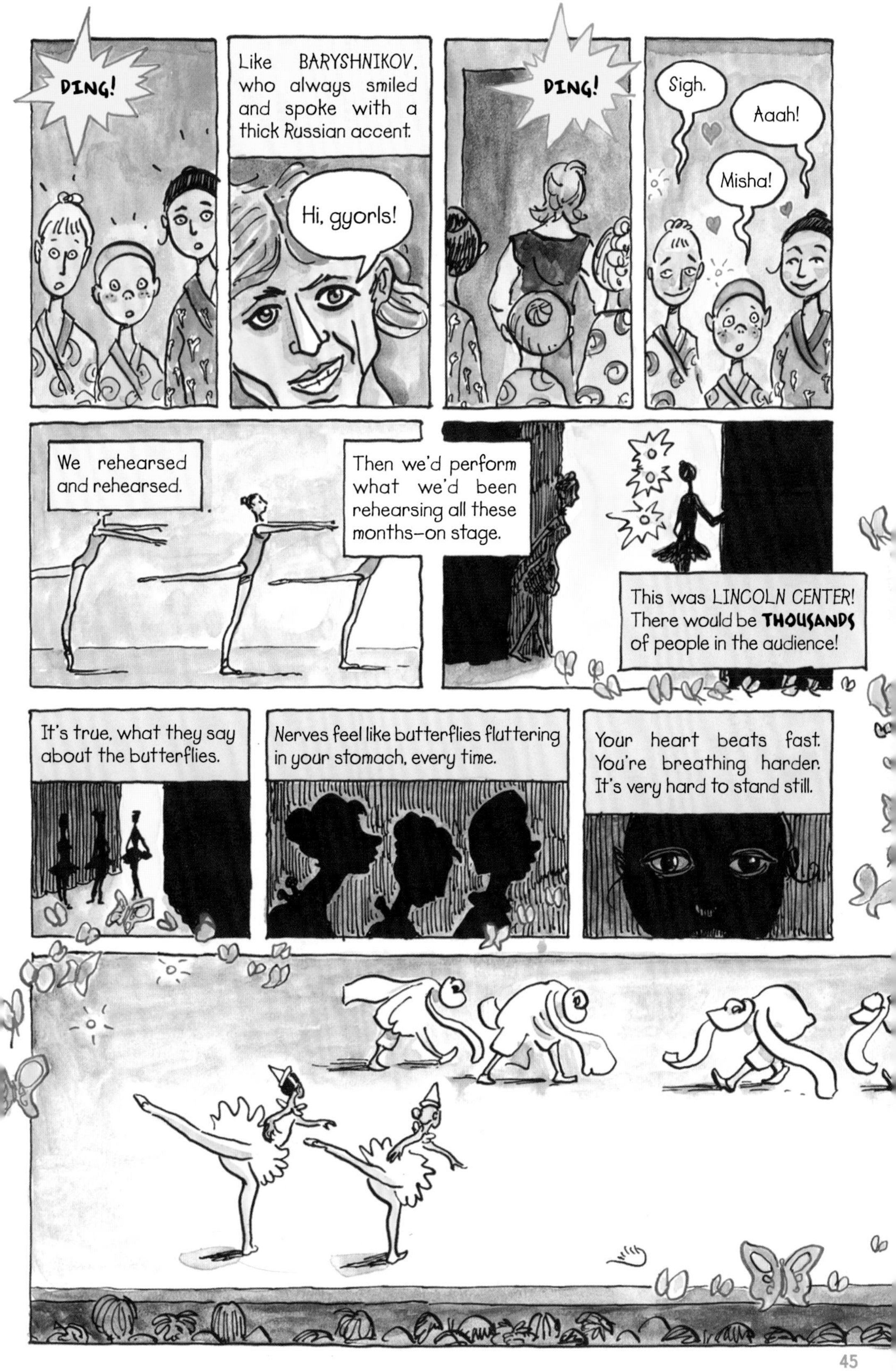
DING!
Like BARYSHNIKOV, who always smiled and spoke with a thick Russian accent.
Hi, gyorls!
DING!
Sigh.
Aaah!
Misha!
We rehearsed and rehearsed.
Then we'd perform what we'd been rehearsing all these months—on stage.
This was LINCOLN CENTER! There would be **THOUSANDS** of people in the audience!
It's true, what they say about the butterflies.
Nerves feel like butterflies fluttering in your stomach, every time.
Your heart beats fast. You're breathing harder. It's very hard to stand still.

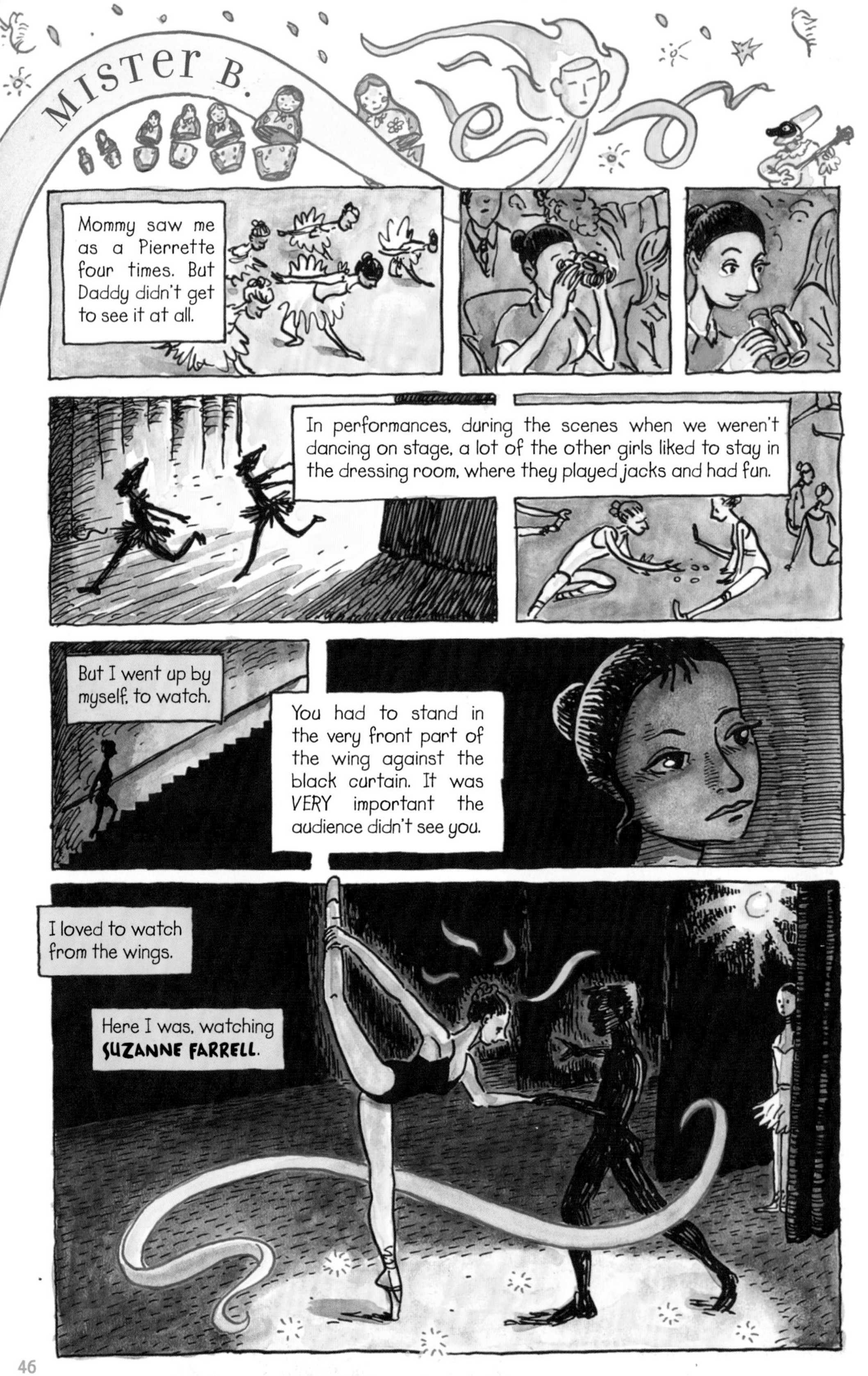
MISTER B.
Mommy saw me as a Pierrette four times. But Daddy didn't get to see it at all.
In performances, during the scenes when we weren't dancing on stage, a lot of the other girls liked to stay in the dressing room, where they played jacks and had fun.
But I went up by myself, to watch.
You had to stand in the very front part of the wing against the black curtain. It was VERY important the audience didn't see you.
I loved to watch from the wings.
Here I was, watching SUZANNE FARRELL.

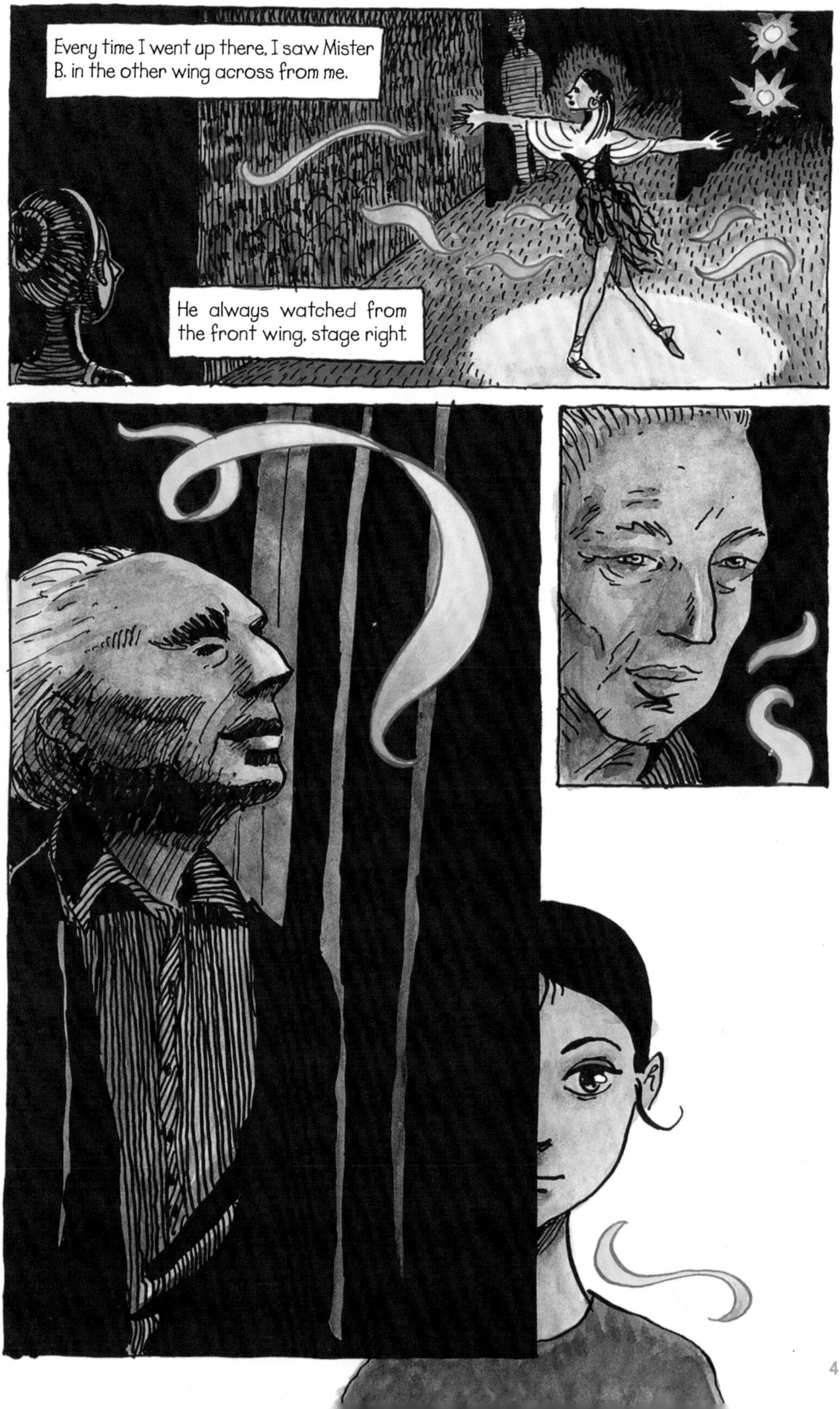
Every time I went up there, I saw Mister B. in the other wing across from me.
He always watched from the front wing, stage right.

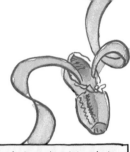

Back to the Barre

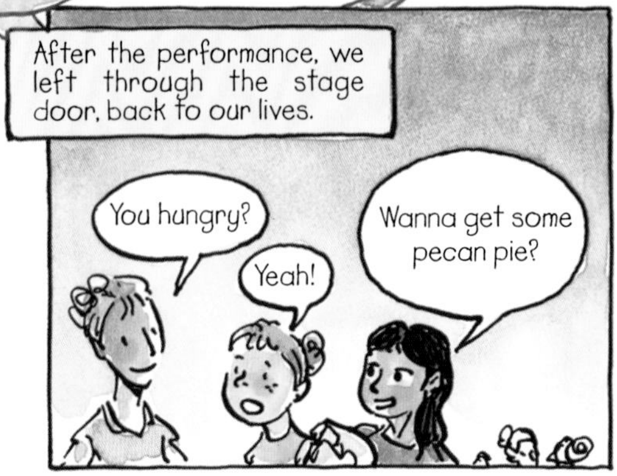
After the performance, we left through the stage door, back to our lives.
You hungry?
Yeah!
Wanna get some pecan pie?

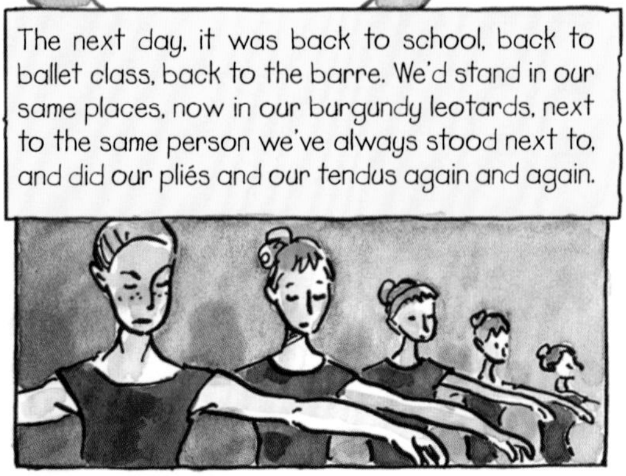
The next day, it was back to school, back to ballet class, back to the barre. We'd stand in our same places, now in our burgundy leotards, next to the same person we've always stood next to, and did our pliés and our tendus again and again.

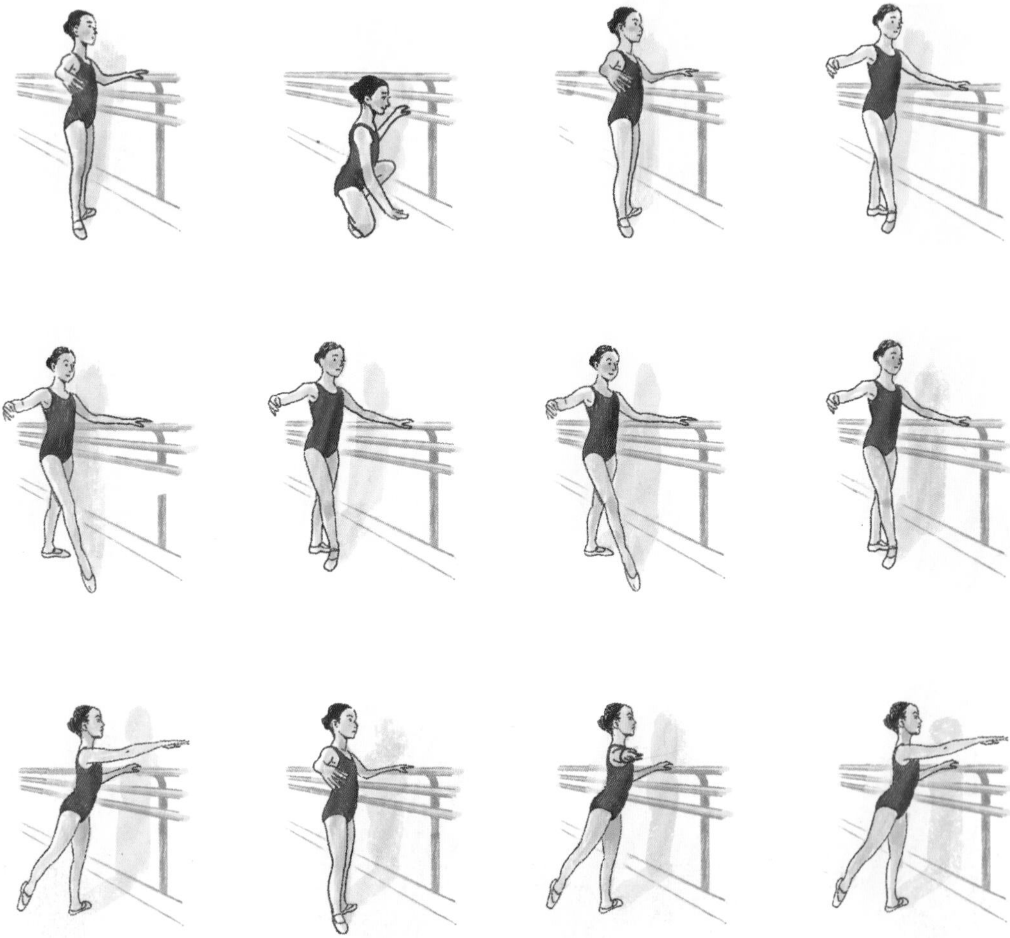

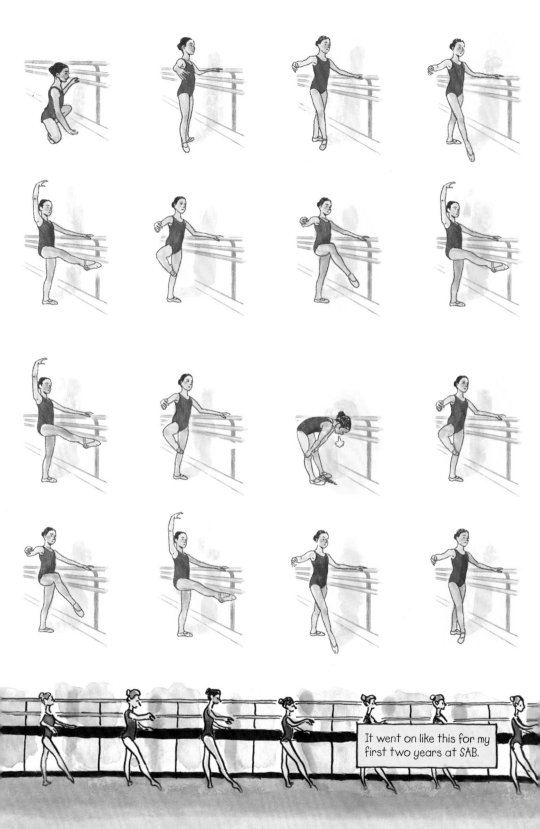

It went on like this for my first two years at SAB.

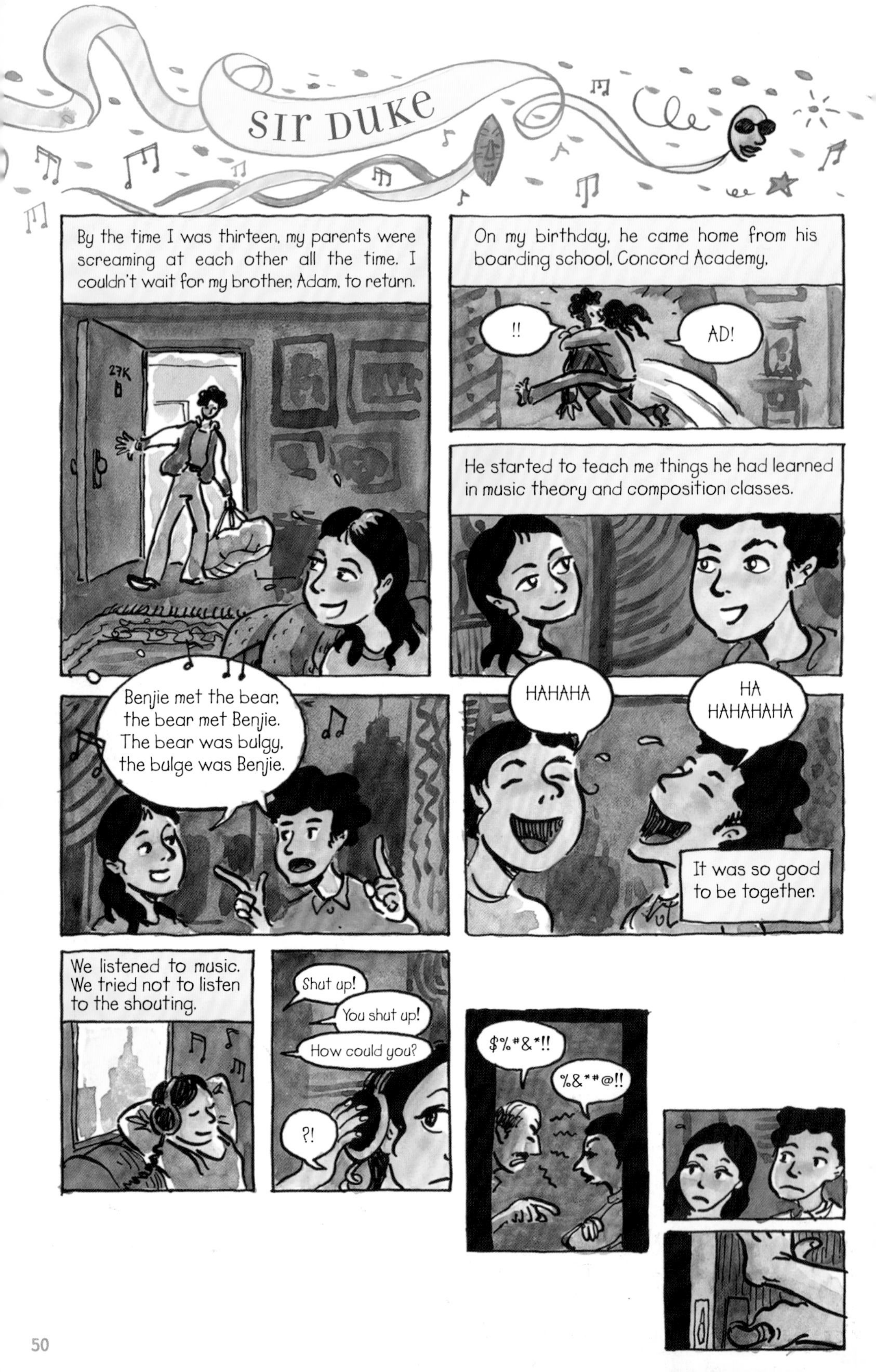
SIR DUKE
By the time I was thirteen, my parents were screaming at each other all the time. I couldn't wait for my brother, Adam, to return.
27K
On my birthday, he came home from his boarding school, Concord Academy.
!!
AD!
He started to teach me things he had learned in music theory and composition classes.
Benjie met the bear, the bear met Benjie. The bear was bulgy, the bulge was Benjie.
HAHAHA
HA HAHAHAHA
It was so good to be together.
We listened to music. We tried not to listen to the shouting.
Shut up!
You shut up!
How could you?
?!
$%*&*!!
%&**@!!

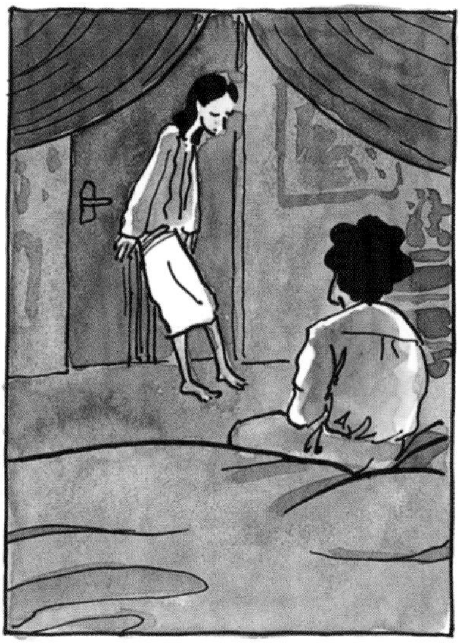

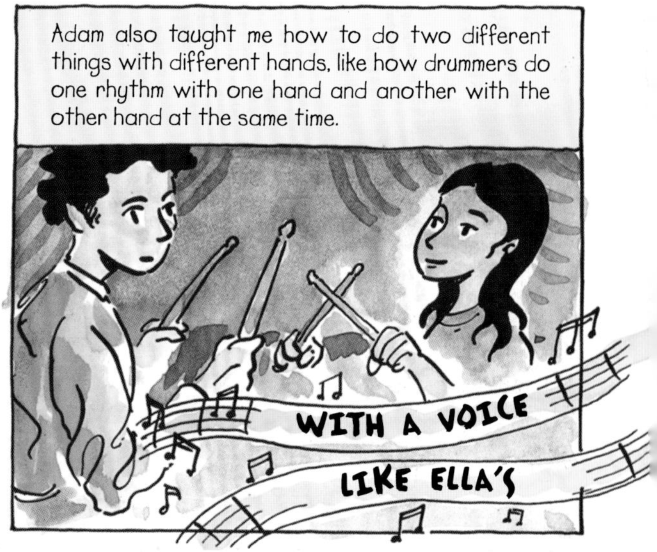
Adam also taught me how to do two different things with different hands, like how drummers do one rhythm with one hand and another with the other hand at the same time.
WITH A VOICE
LIKE ELLA'S

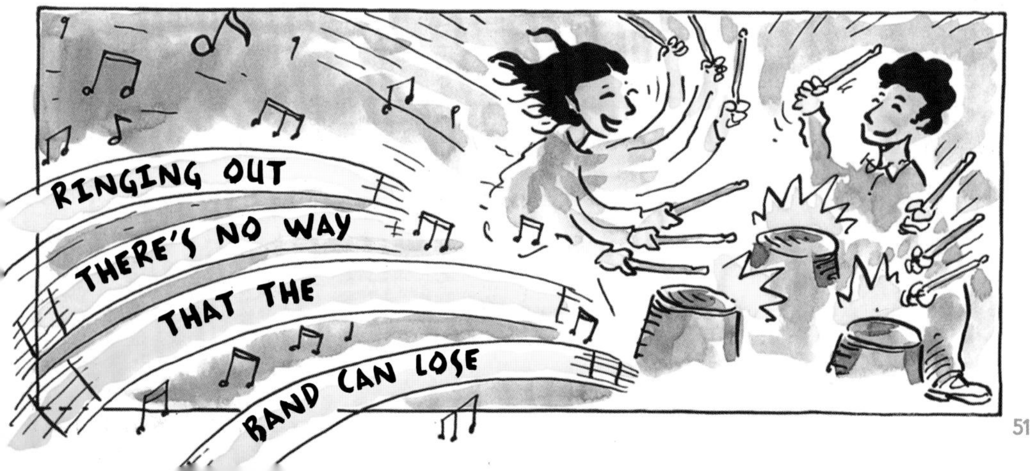
RINGING OUT
THERE'S NO WAY
THAT THE
BAND CAN LOSE

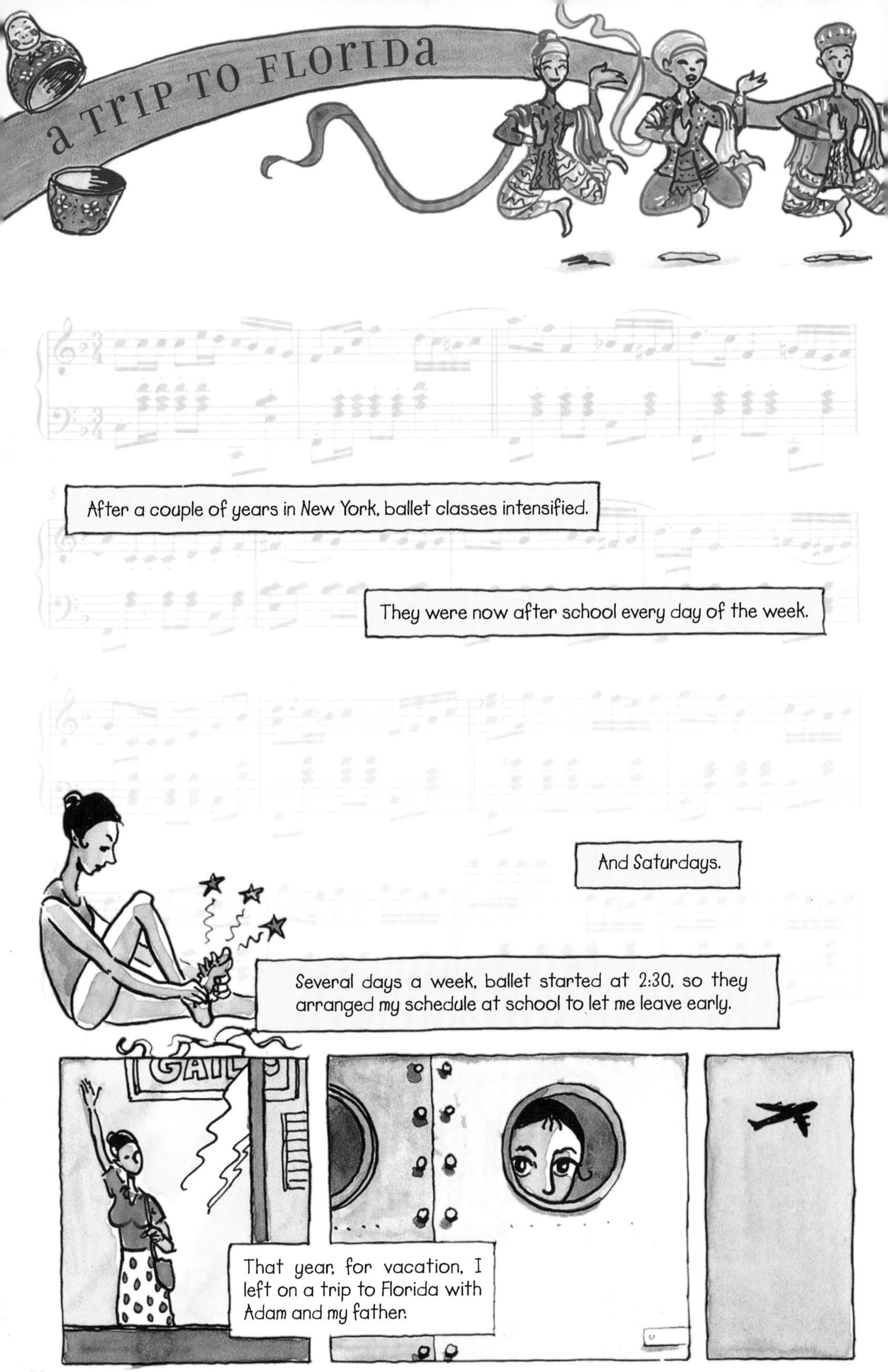
a Trip to Florida
After a couple of years in New York, ballet classes intensified.
They were now after school every day of the week.
And Saturdays.
Several days a week, ballet started at 2:30, so they arranged my schedule at school to let me leave early.
That year, for vacation, I left on a trip to Florida with Adam and my father.

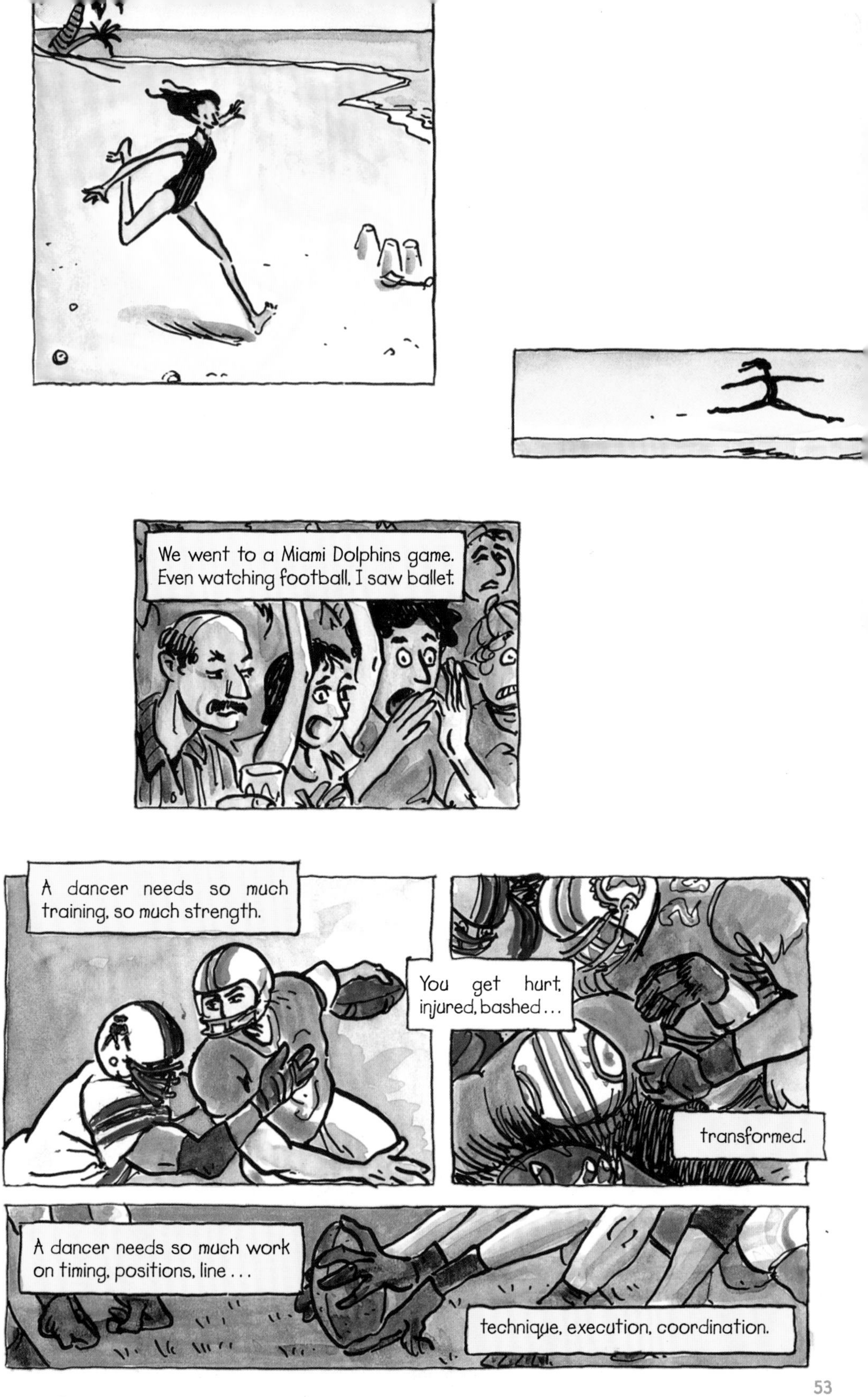
We went to a Miami Dolphins game. Even watching football, I saw ballet.
A dancer needs so much training, so much strength.
You get hurt, injured, bashed . . .
transformed.
A dancer needs so much work on timing, positions, line . . .
technique, execution, coordination.

And then . . .

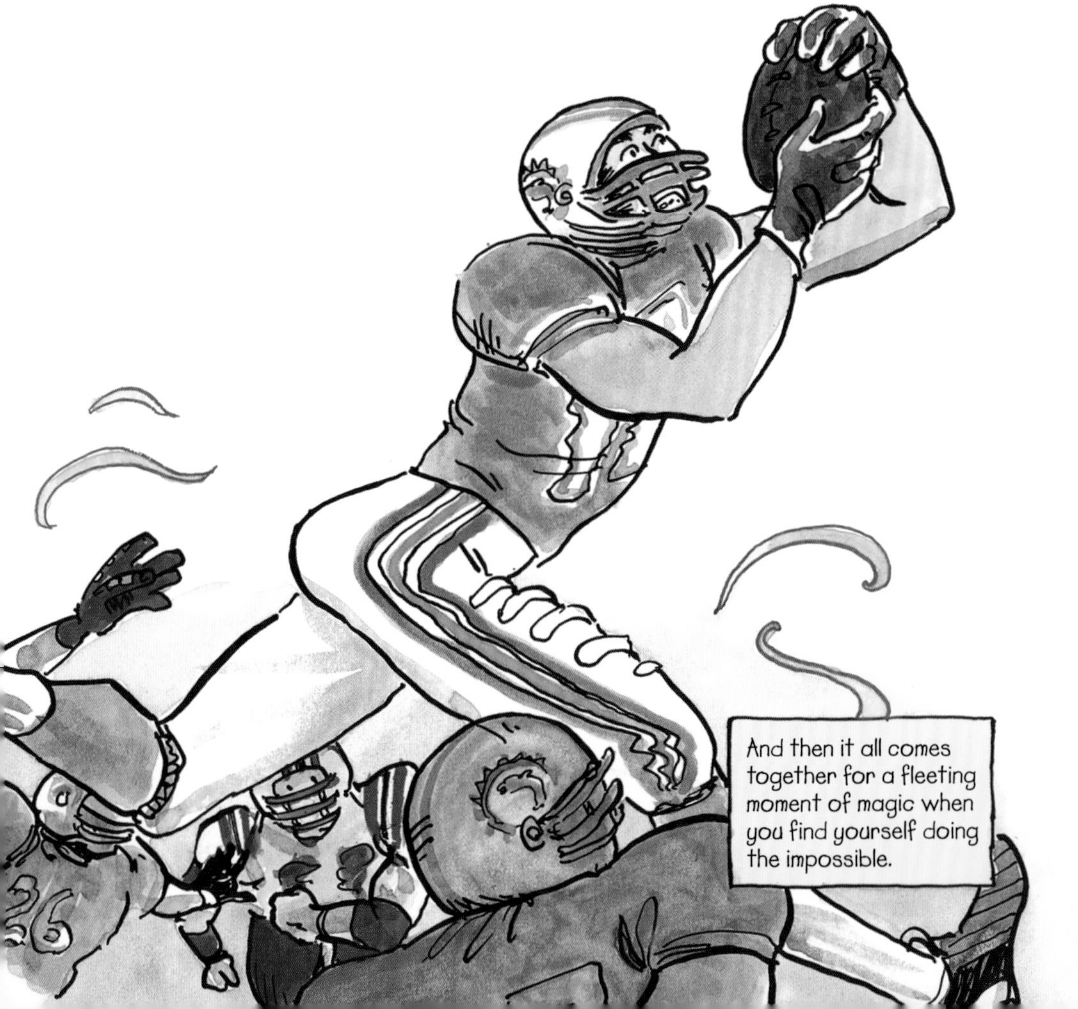
And then it all comes together for a fleeting moment of magic when you find yourself doing the impossible.

We also saw my father's relatives there, for dinner.

Her boobs are huge!

It runs in my family!

Oh no. What if mine keep growing and growing and growing!

You really can't be a ballet dancer and have huge breasts!

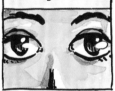

I thought maybe I should tie gauze around them at night, hoping that might contain them a bit at least.

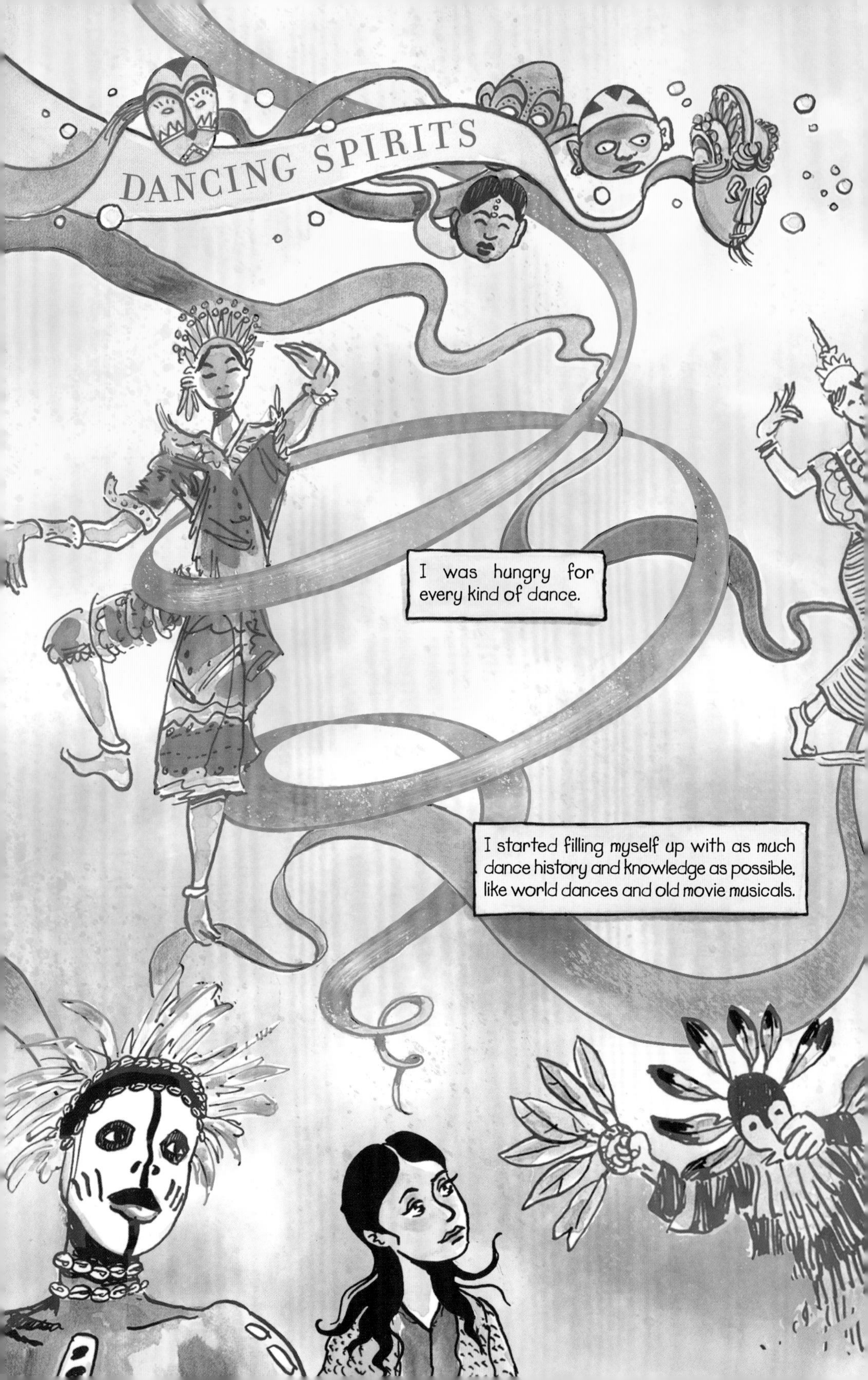
DANCING SPIRITS
I was hungry for every kind of dance.
I started filling myself up with as much dance history and knowledge as possible, like world dances and old movie musicals.

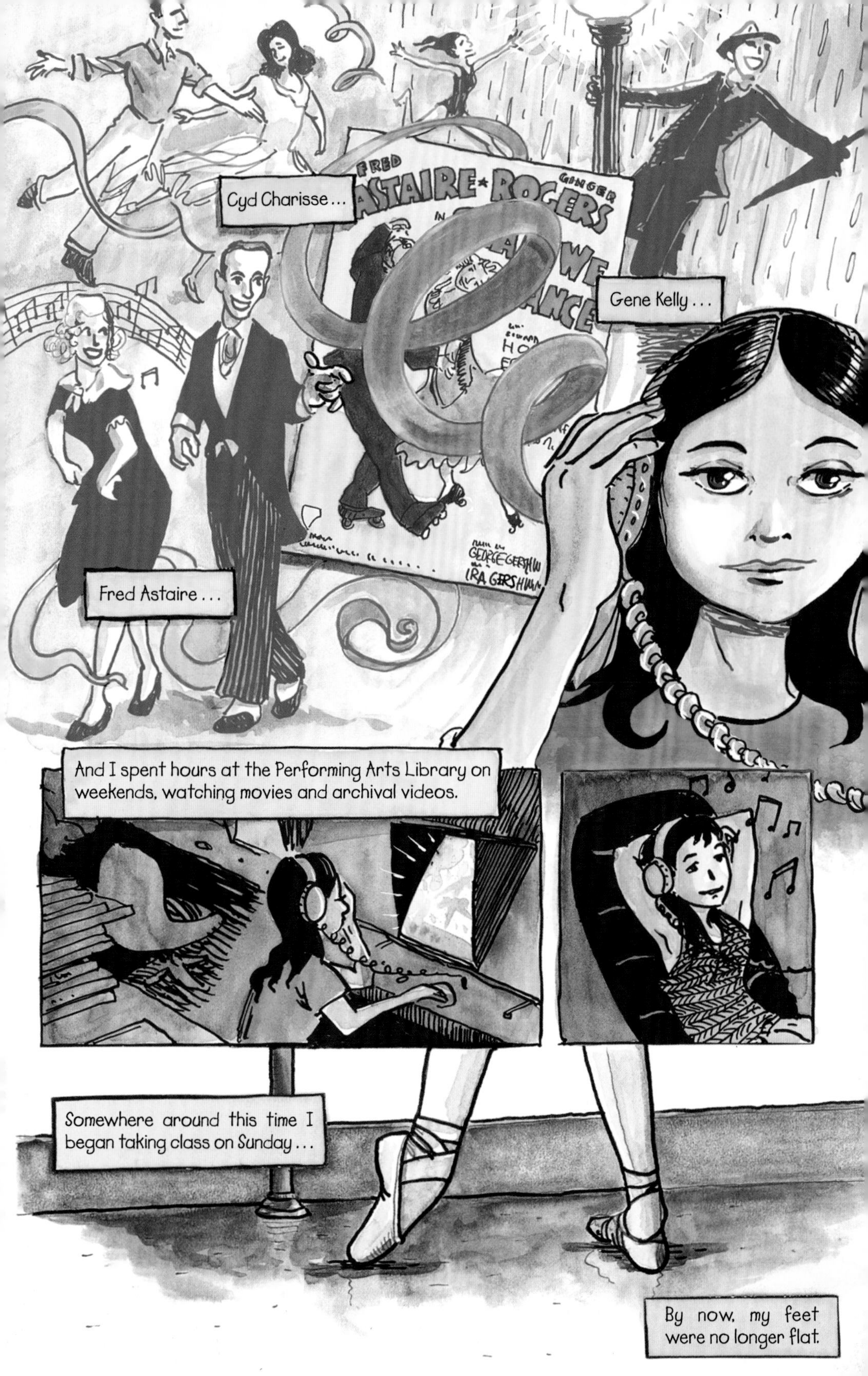
Cyd Charisse . . .
FRED ASTAIRE ★ ROGERS GINGER
Gene Kelly . . .
GEORGE GERSHWIN
IRA GERSHWIN
Fred Astaire . . .
And I spent hours at the Performing Arts Library on weekends, watching movies and archival videos.
Somewhere around this time I began taking class on Sunday . . .
By now, my feet were no longer flat.

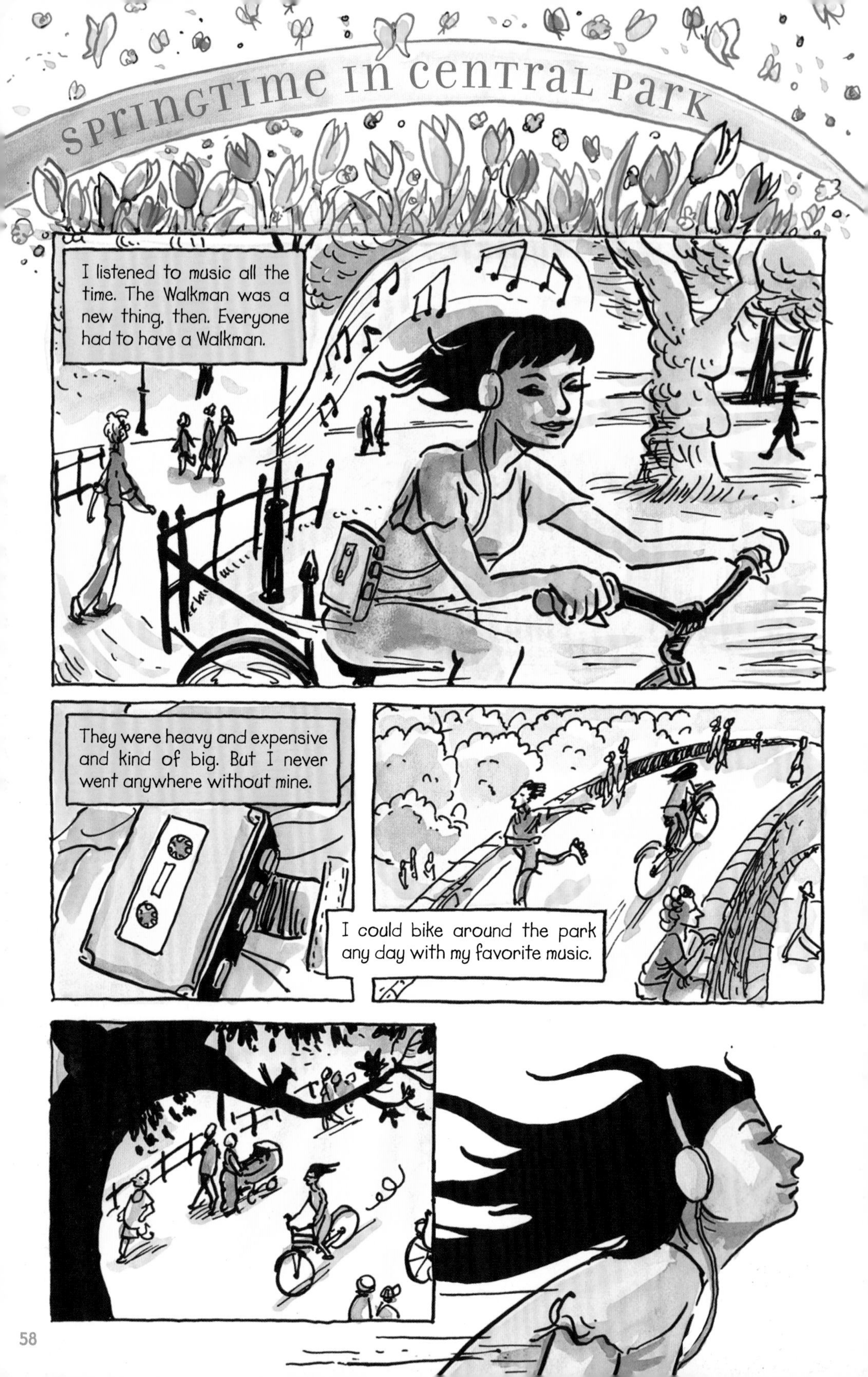
Springtime in Central Park
I listened to music all the time. The Walkman was a new thing, then. Everyone had to have a Walkman.
They were heavy and expensive and kind of big. But I never went anywhere without mine.
I could bike around the park any day with my favorite music.

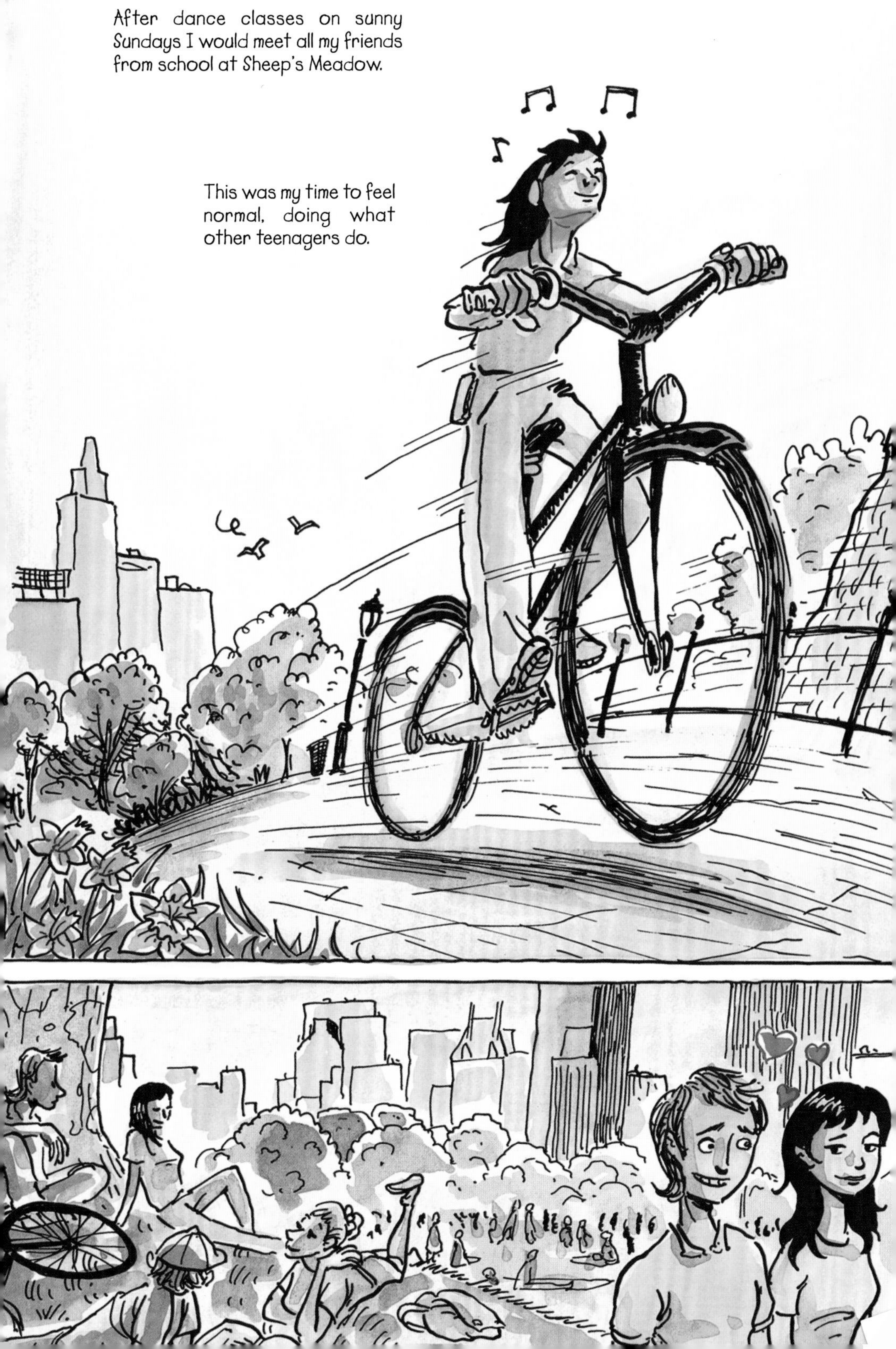
After dance classes on sunny Sundays I would meet all my friends from school at Sheep's Meadow.
This was my time to feel normal, doing what other teenagers do.

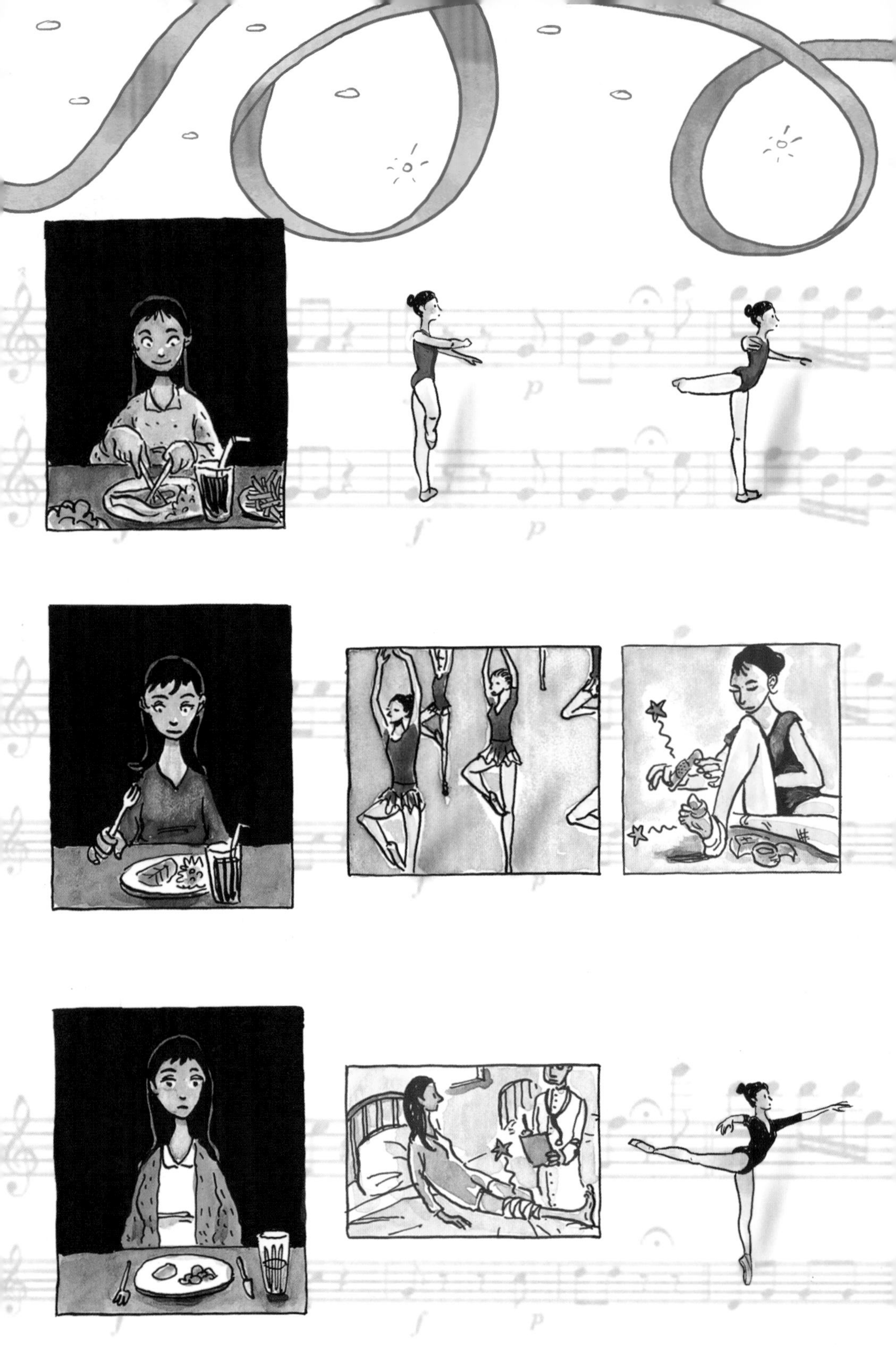

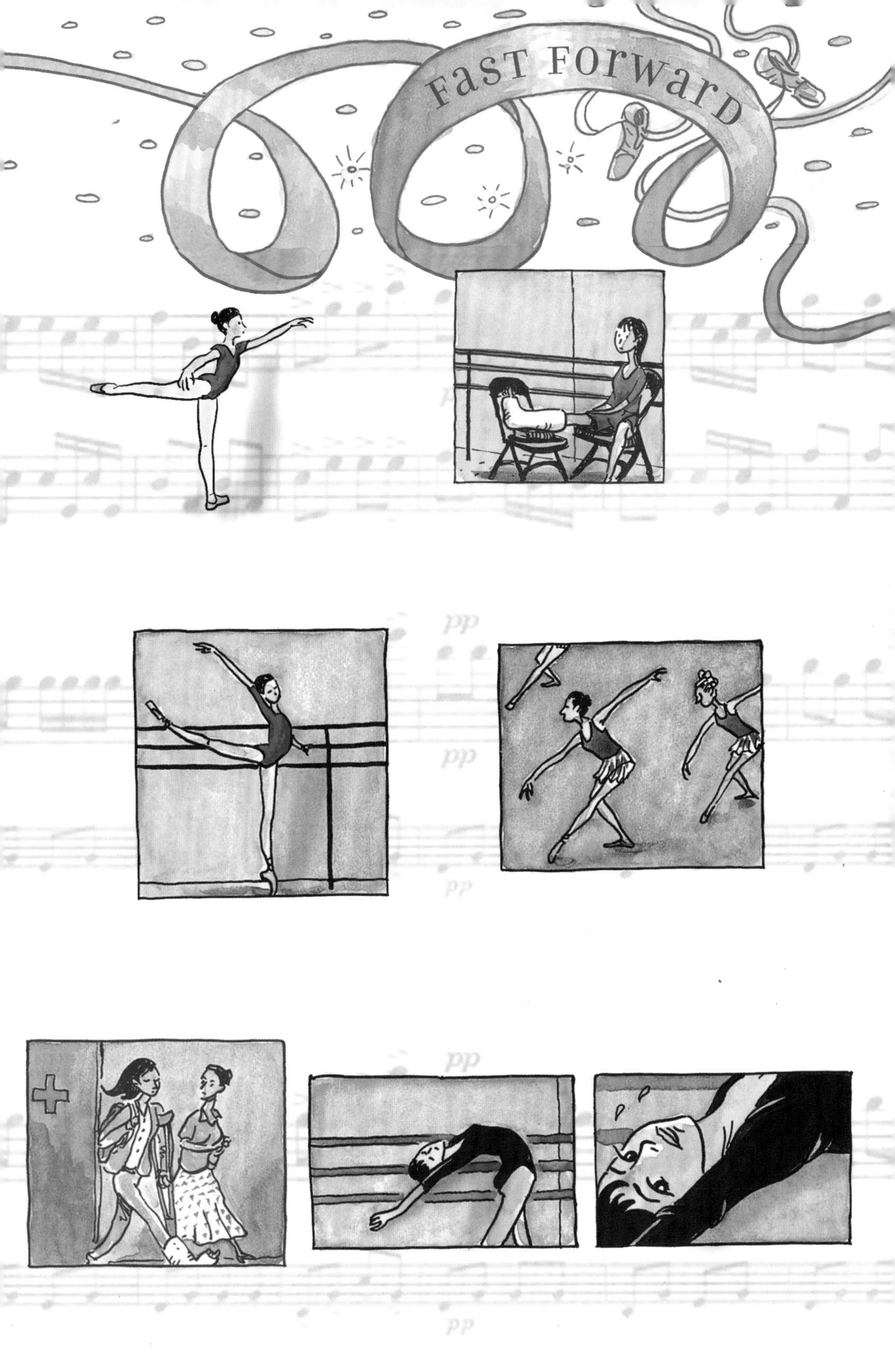
Fast Forward
pp
pp
pp
pp
pp

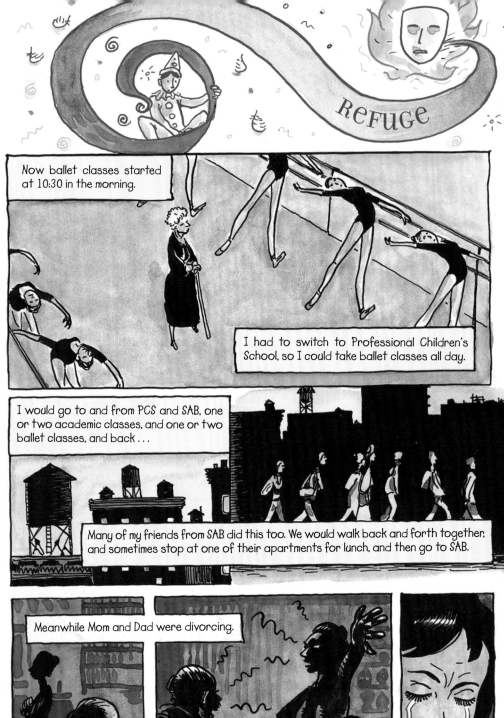

REFUGE

Now ballet classes started at 10:30 in the morning.

I had to switch to Professional Children's School, so I could take ballet classes all day.

I would go to and from PCS and SAB, one or two academic classes, and one or two ballet classes, and back . . .

Many of my friends from SAB did this too. We would walk back and forth together, and sometimes stop at one of their apartments for lunch, and then go to SAB.

Meanwhile Mom and Dad were divorcing.

There was no peace at home.

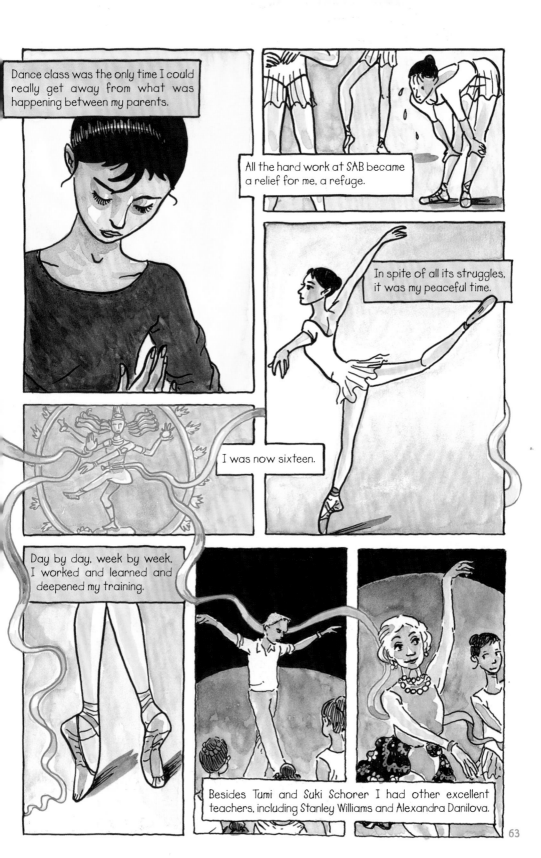

Dance class was the only time I could really get away from what was happening between my parents.

All the hard work at SAB became a relief for me, a refuge.

In spite of all its struggles, it was my peaceful time.

I was now sixteen.

Day by day, week by week, I worked and learned and deepened my training.

Besides Tumi and Suki Schorer I had other excellent teachers, including Stanley Williams and Alexandra Danilova.

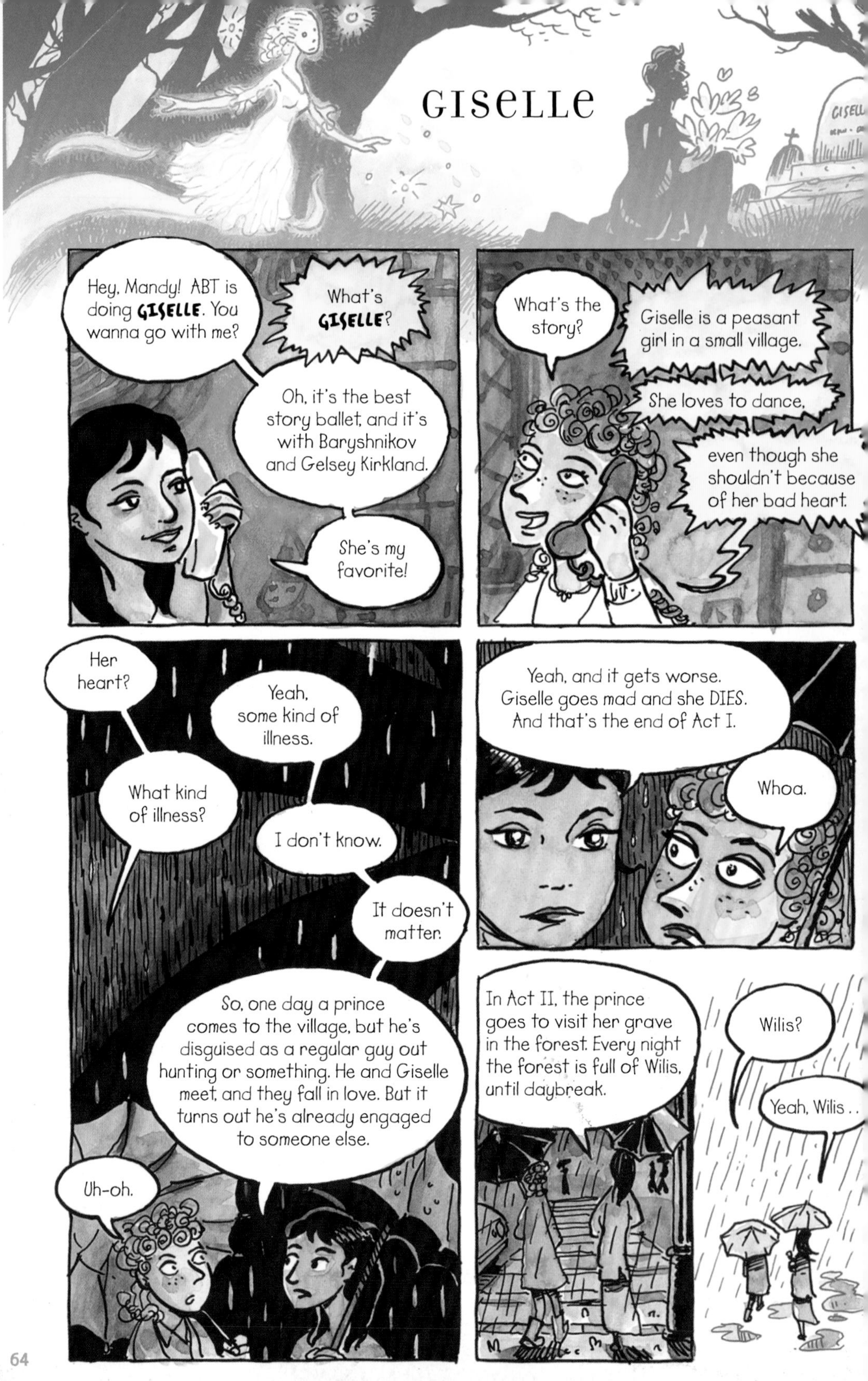
GISELLE
Hey, Mandy! ABT is doing GISELLE. You wanna go with me?
What's GISELLE?
Oh, it's the best story ballet, and it's with Baryshnikov and Gelsey Kirkland.
She's my favorite!
What's the story?
Giselle is a peasant girl in a small village.
She loves to dance,
even though she shouldn't because of her bad heart.
Her heart?
Yeah, some kind of illness.
What kind of illness?
I don't know.
It doesn't matter.
So, one day a prince comes to the village, but he's disguised as a regular guy out hunting or something. He and Giselle meet, and they fall in love. But it turns out he's already engaged to someone else.
Uh-oh.
Yeah, and it gets worse. Giselle goes mad and she DIES. And that's the end of Act I.
Whoa.
In Act II, the prince goes to visit her grave in the forest. Every night the forest is full of Wilis, until daybreak.
Wilis?
Yeah, Wilis . . .

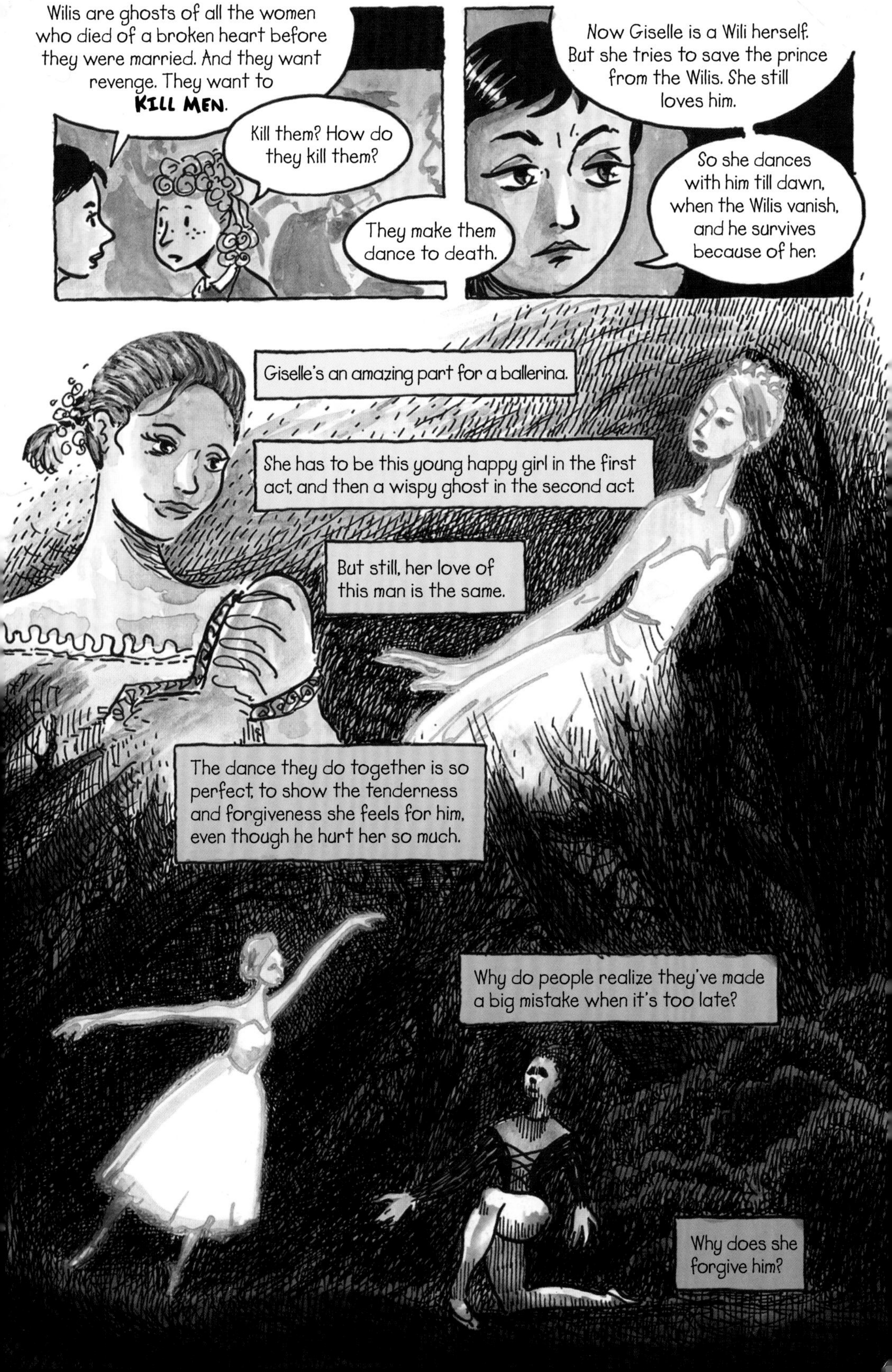
Wilis are ghosts of all the women who died of a broken heart before they were married. And they want revenge. They want to KILL MEN.
Kill them? How do they kill them?
They make them dance to death.
Now Giselle is a Wili herself. But she tries to save the prince from the Wilis. She still loves him.
So she dances with him till dawn, when the Wilis vanish, and he survives because of her.
Giselle's an amazing part for a ballerina.
She has to be this young happy girl in the first act, and then a wispy ghost in the second act.
But still, her love of this man is the same.
The dance they do together is so perfect, to show the tenderness and forgiveness she feels for him, even though he hurt her so much.
Why do people realize they've made a big mistake when it's too late?
Why does she forgive him?

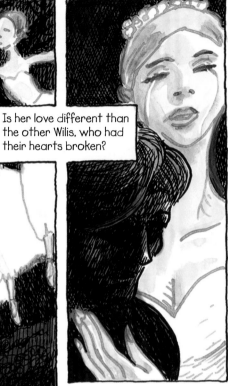

Is her love different than the other Wilis, who had their hearts broken?

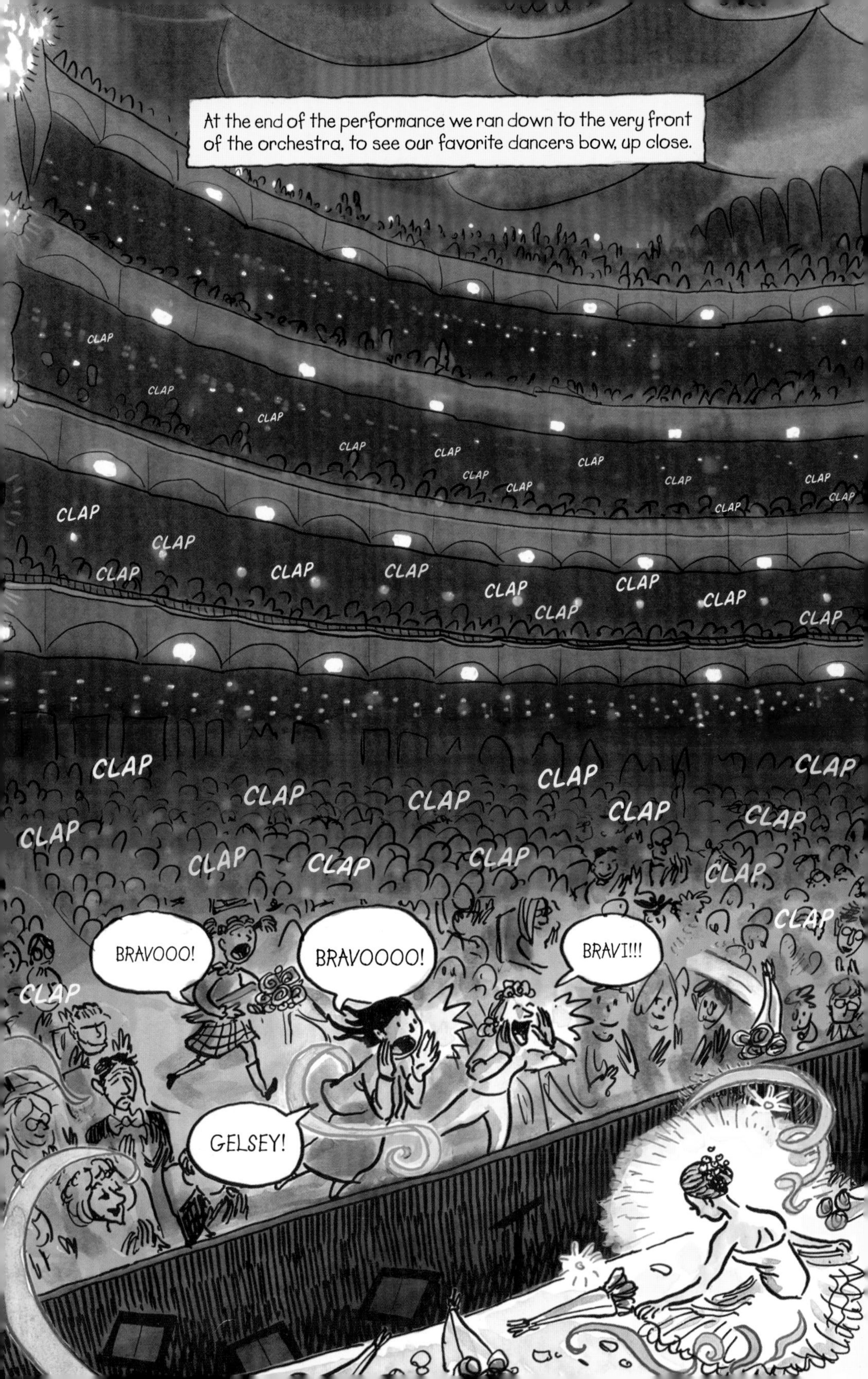
At the end of the performance we ran down to the very front of the orchestra, to see our favorite dancers bow, up close.
CLAP CLAP CLAP CLAP CLAP CLAP CLAP CLAP CLAP CLAP CLAP CLAP CLAP
CLAP CLAP CLAP CLAP CLAP CLAP CLAP CLAP CLAP CLAP
CLAP CLAP CLAP CLAP CLAP CLAP CLAP CLAP CLAP CLAP CLAP CLAP CLAP CLAP CLAP
BRAVOOO!
BRAVOOOO!
BRAVI!!!
GELSEY!

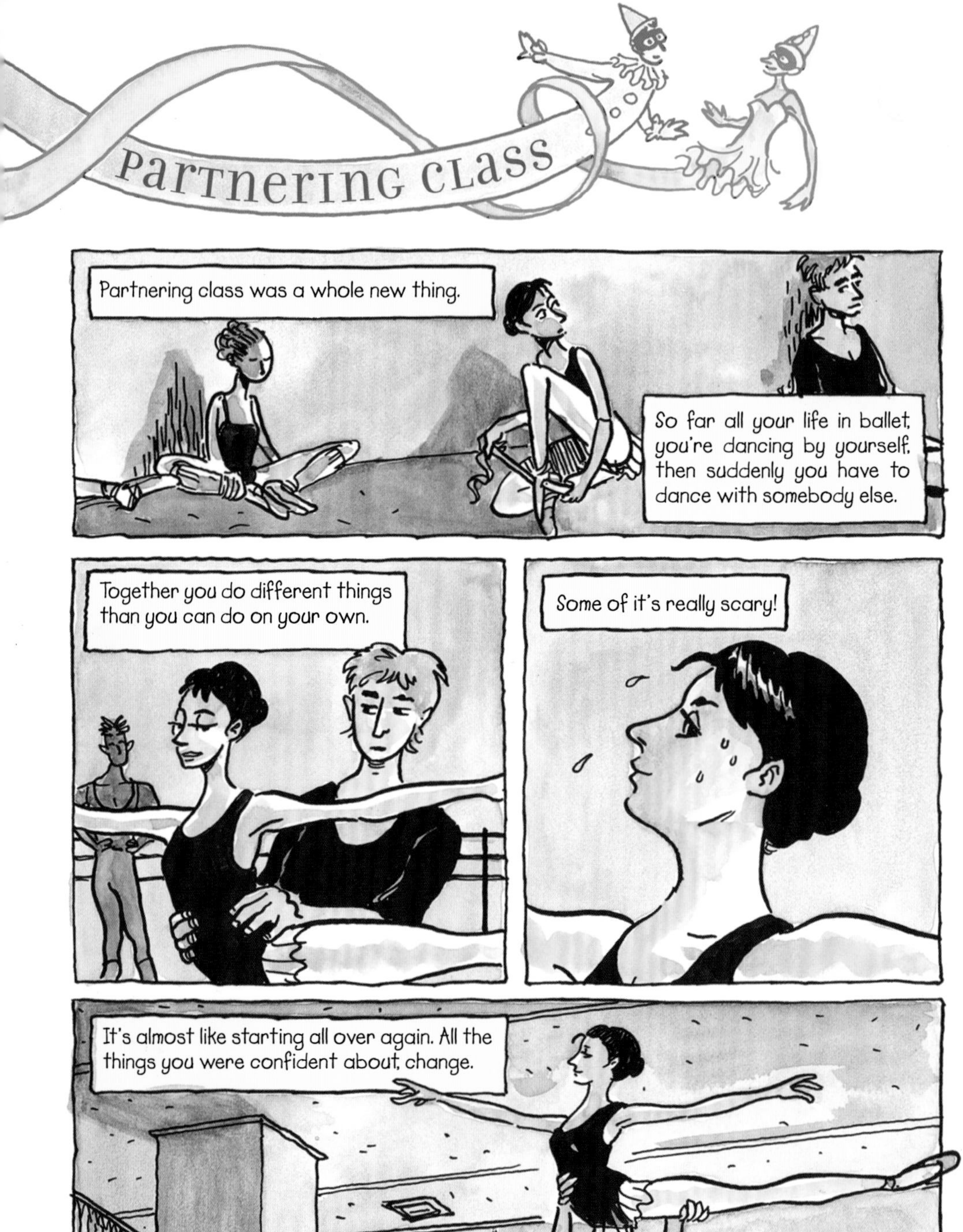
Partnering Class
Partnering class was a whole new thing.
So far all your life in ballet, you're dancing by yourself, then suddenly you have to dance with somebody else.
Together you do different things than you can do on your own.
Some of it's really scary!
It's almost like starting all over again. All the things you were confident about, change.

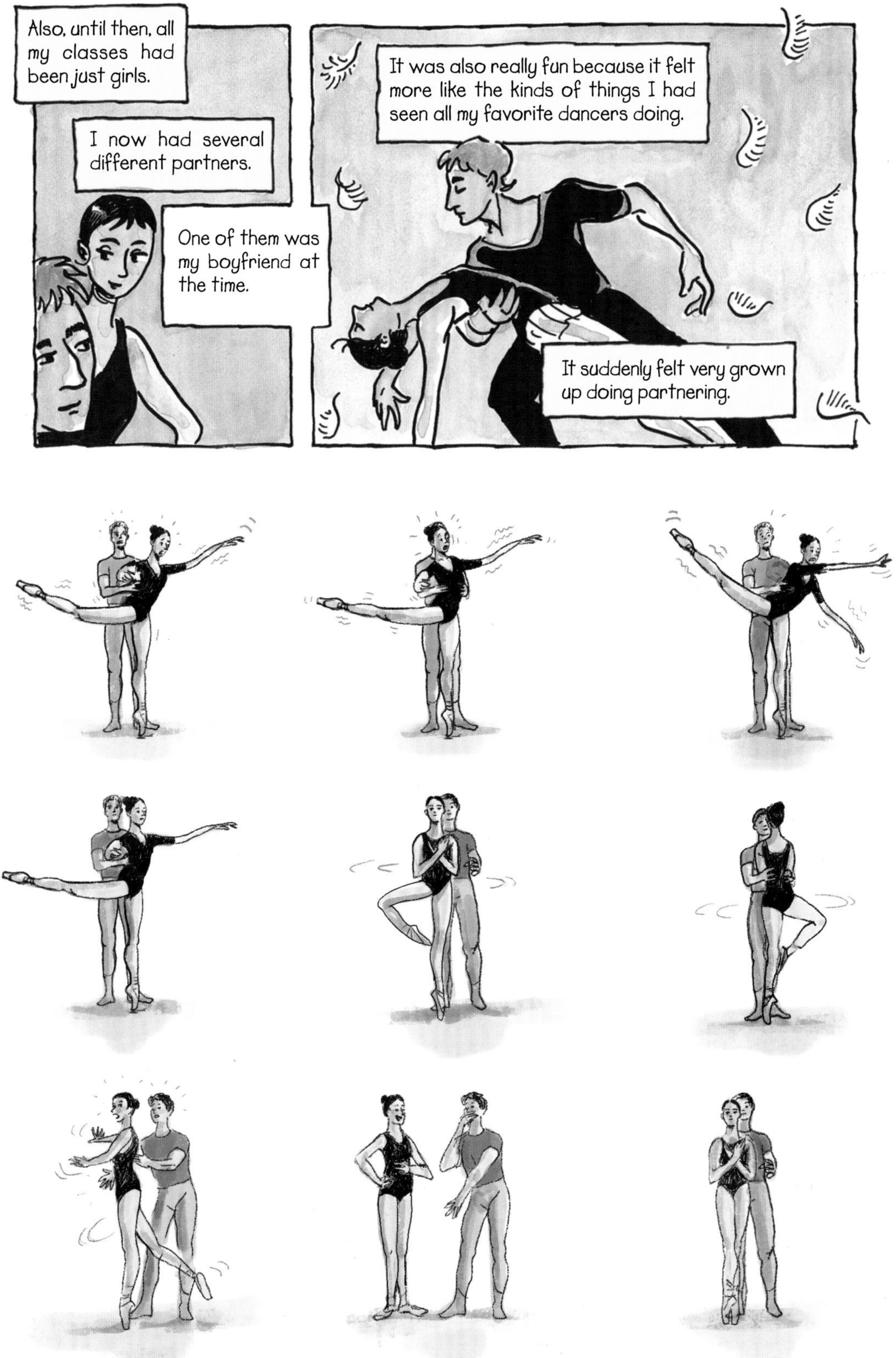
Also, until then, all my classes had been just girls.
I now had several different partners.
One of them was my boyfriend at the time.
It was also really fun because it felt more like the kinds of things I had seen all my favorite dancers doing.
It suddenly felt very grown up doing partnering.

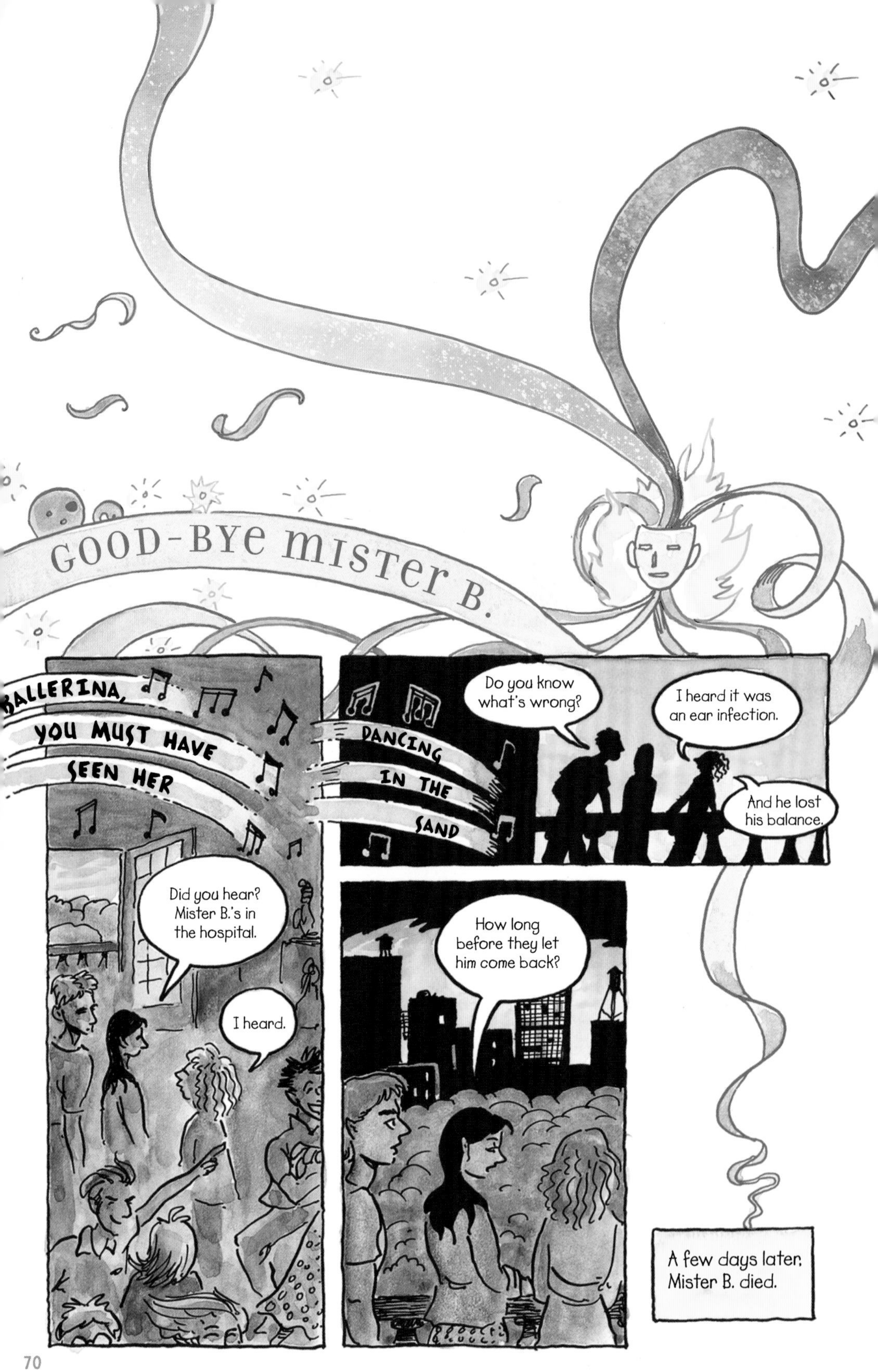
GOOD-BYE MISTER B.
BALLERINA, YOU MUST HAVE SEEN HER
DANCING IN THE SAND
Did you hear? Mister B.'s in the hospital.
I heard.
Do you know what's wrong?
I heard it was an ear infection.
And he lost his balance.
How long before they let him come back?
A few days later, Mister B. died.

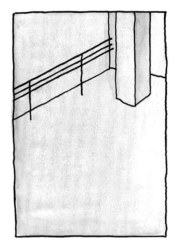

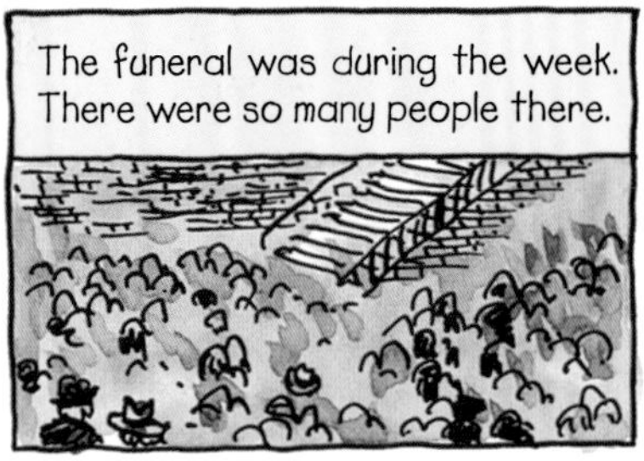
The funeral was during the week. There were so many people there.

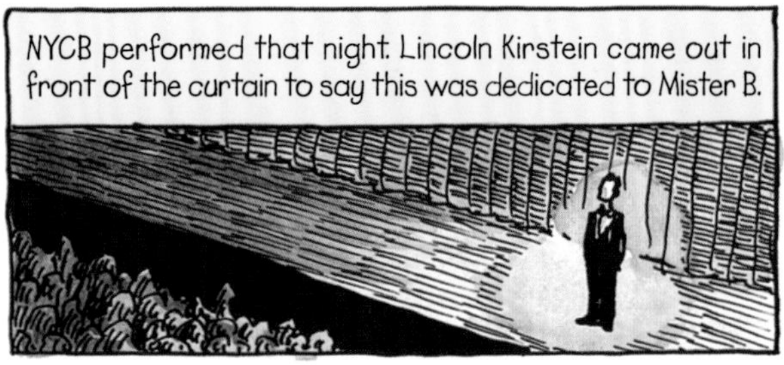
NYCB performed that night. Lincoln Kirstein came out in front of the curtain to say this was dedicated to Mister B.

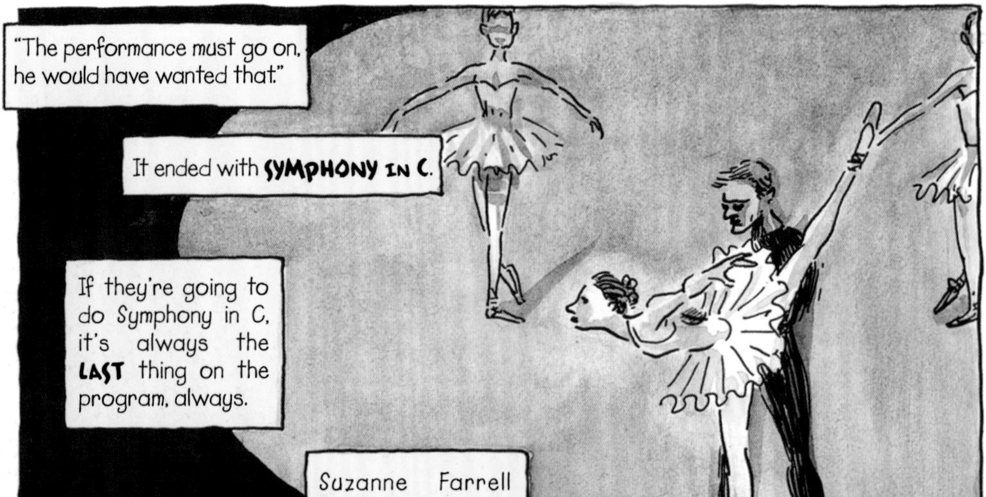
"The performance must go on, he would have wanted that."
It ended with SYMPHONY IN C.
If they're going to do Symphony in C, it's always the LAST thing on the program, always.
Suzanne Farrell was dancing in the second movement, the slow movement.

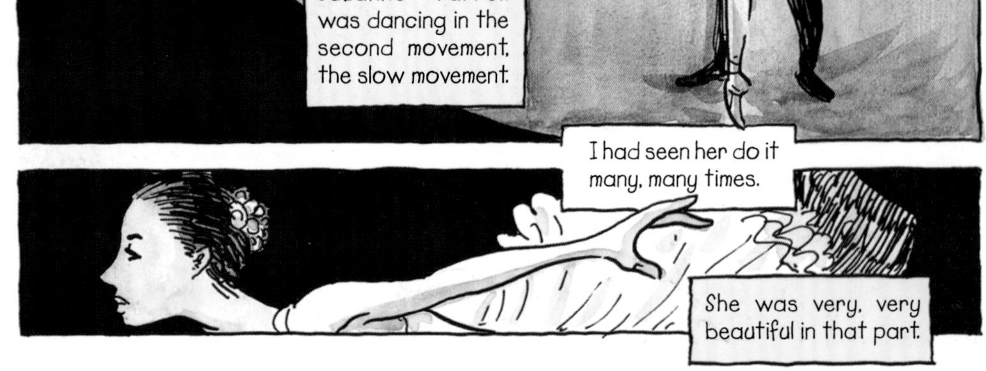
I had seen her do it many, many times.
She was very, very beautiful in that part.

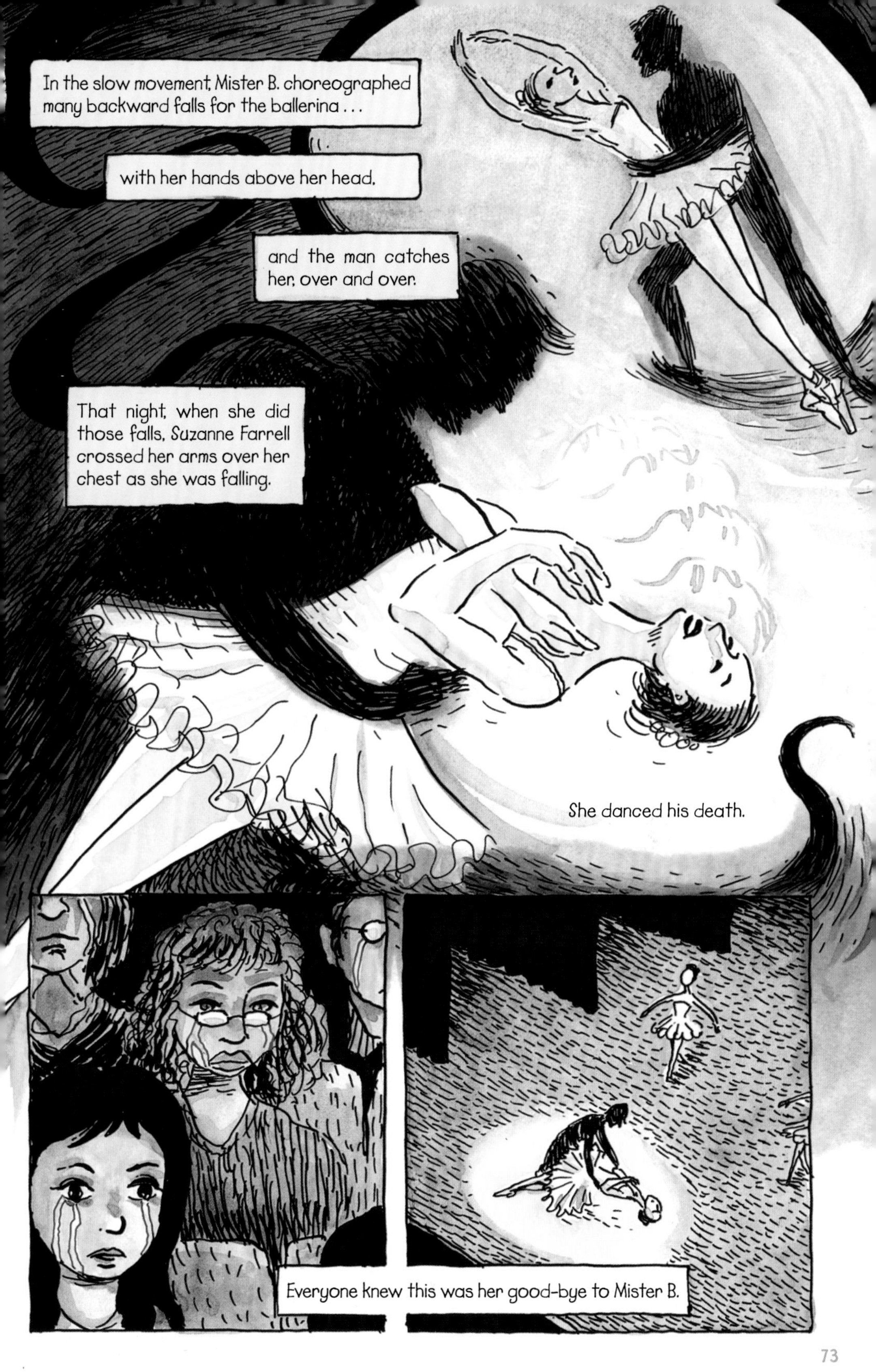
In the slow movement, Mister B. choreographed many backward falls for the ballerina . . .
with her hands above her head,
and the man catches her, over and over.
That night, when she did those falls, Suzanne Farrell crossed her arms over her chest as she was falling.
She danced his death.
Everyone knew this was her good-bye to Mister B.

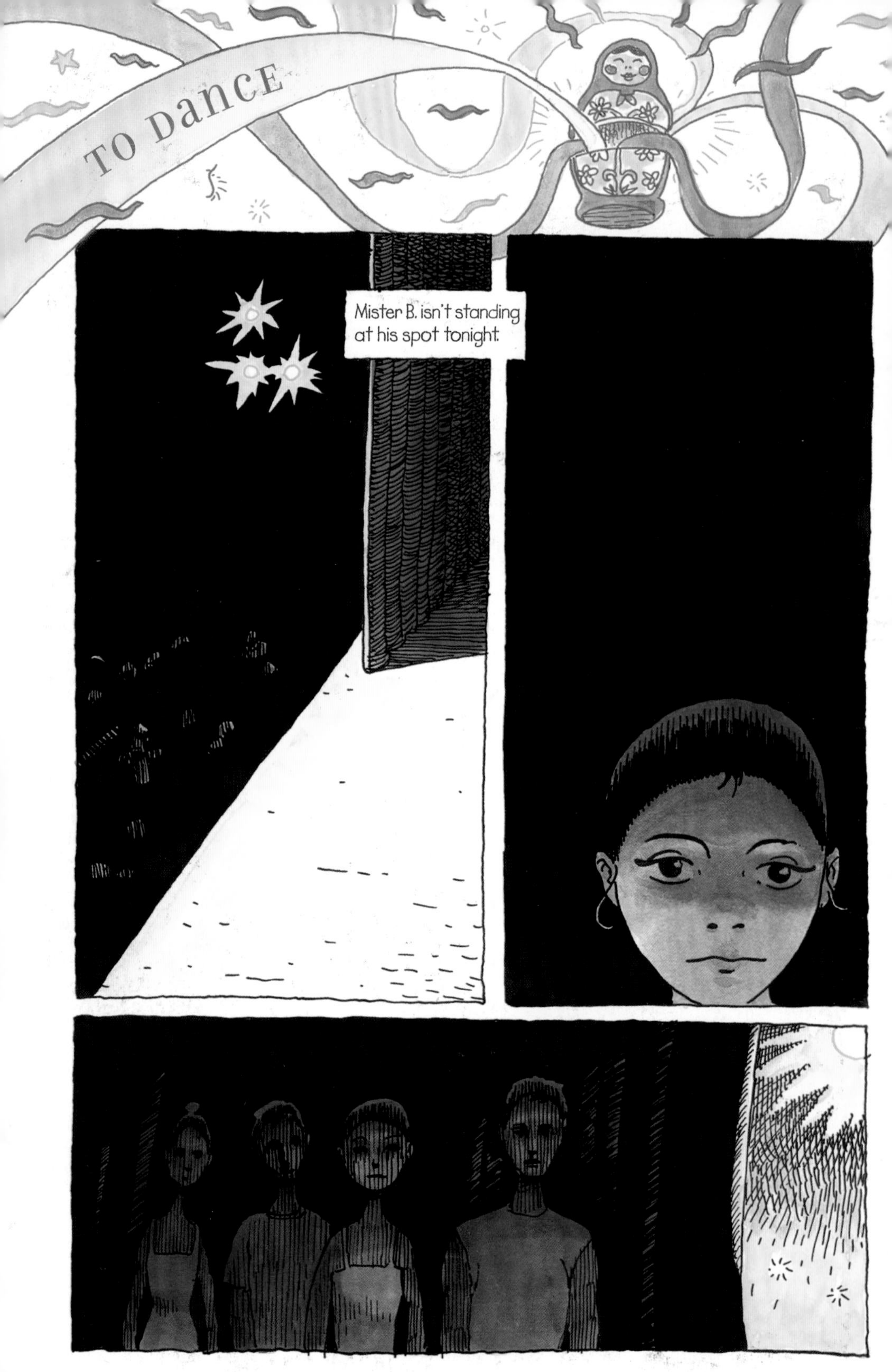
TO DANCE
Mister B. isn't standing at his spot tonight.

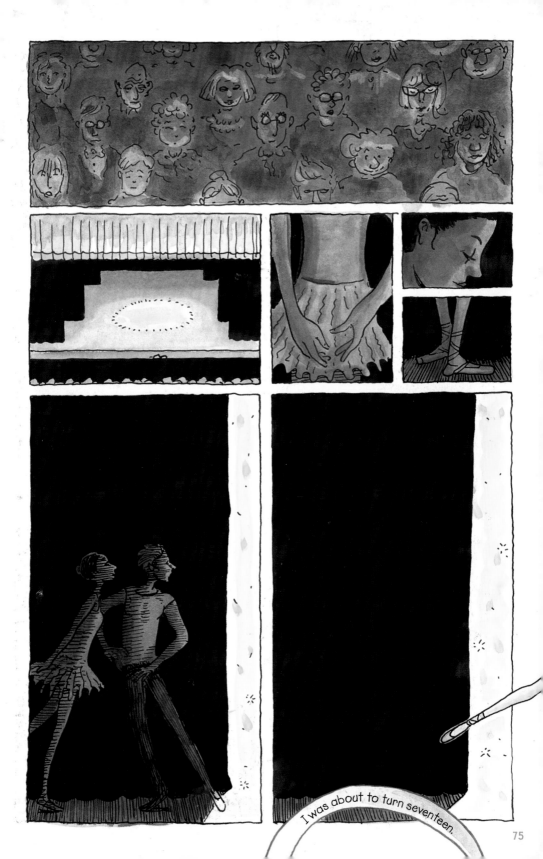

I was about to turn seventeen.

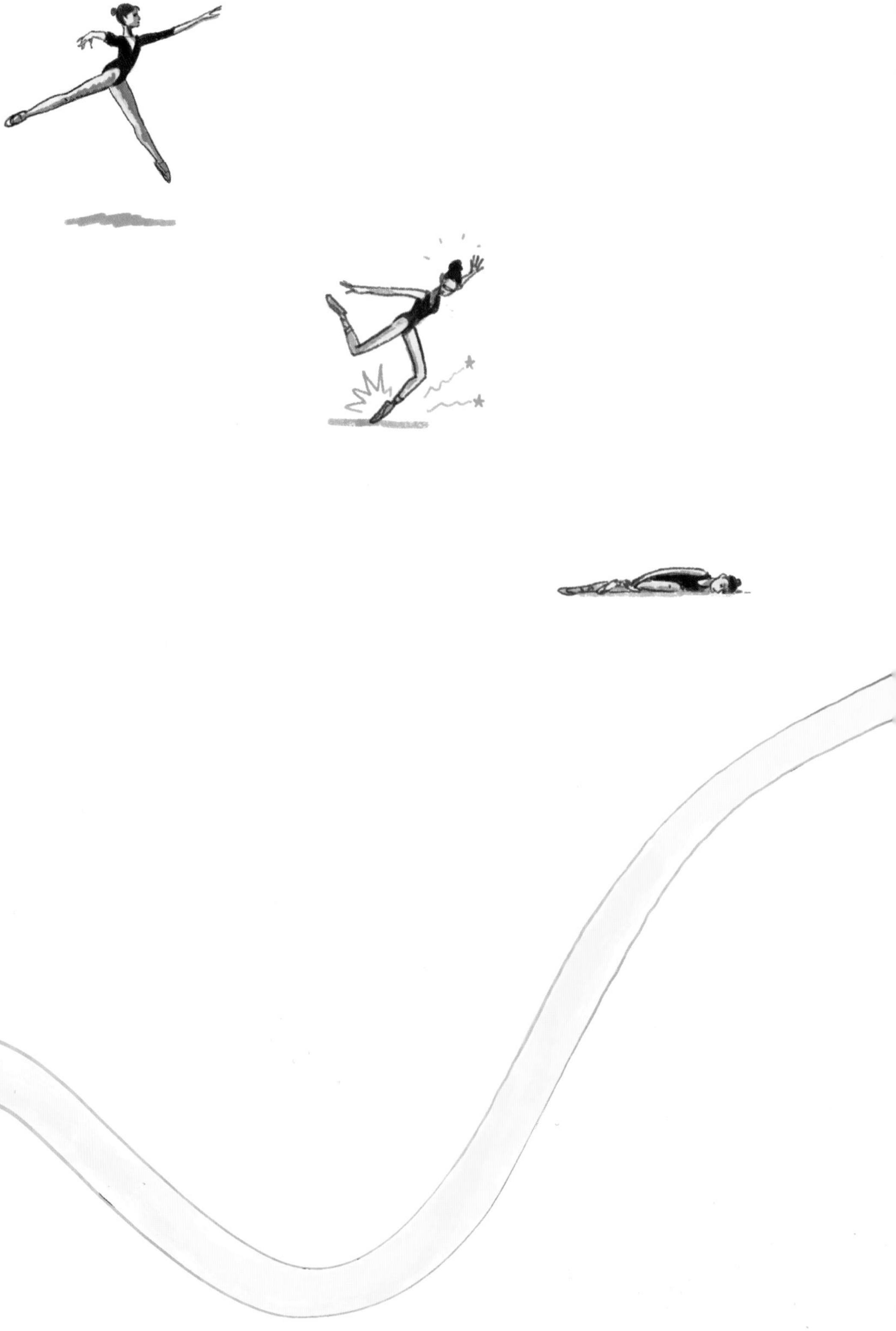

At eighteen I stopped dancing.

I had a terrible ankle injury the year before.

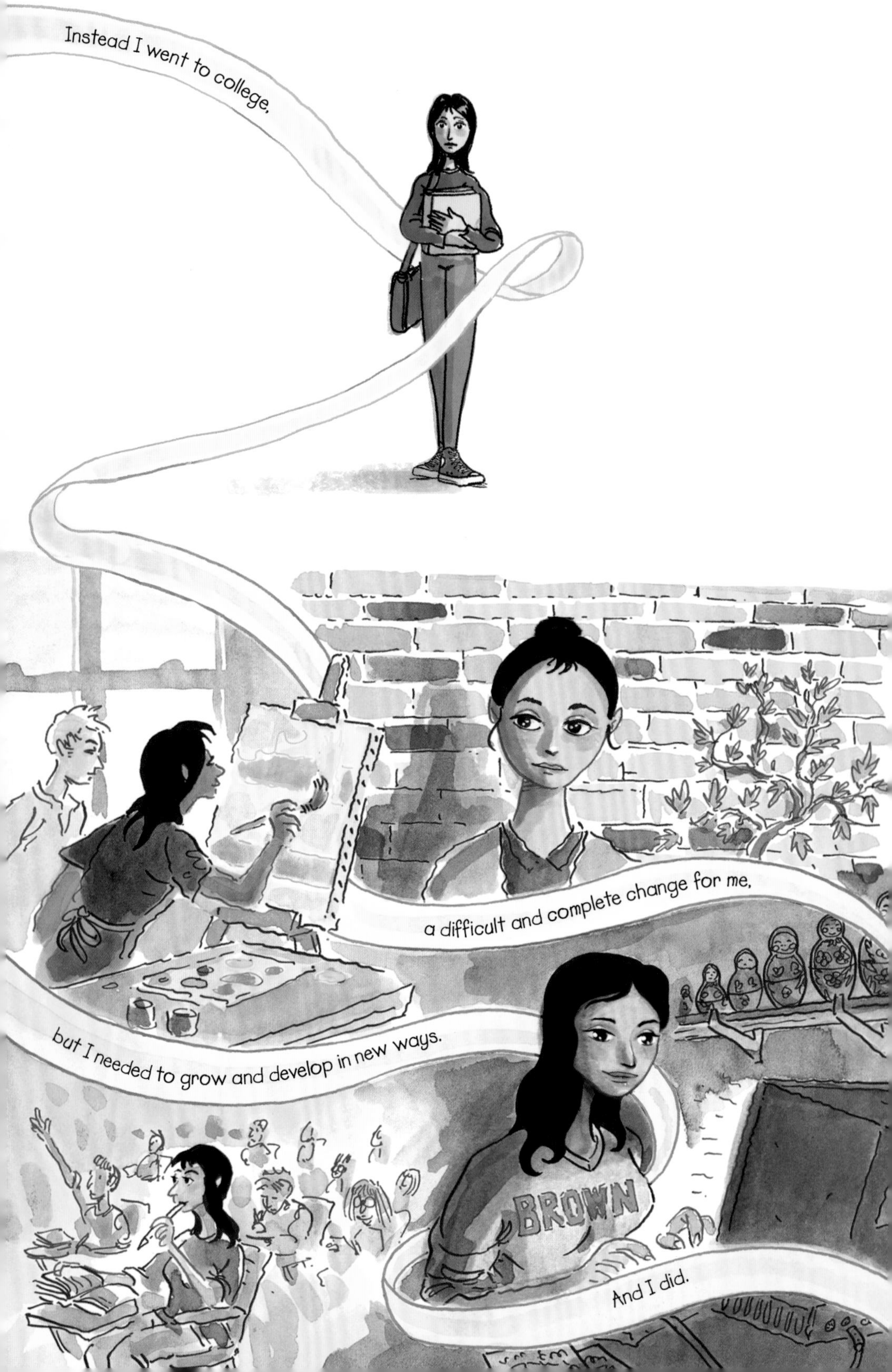
Instead I went to college,
a difficult and complete change for me,
but I needed to grow and develop in new ways.
BROWN
And I did.

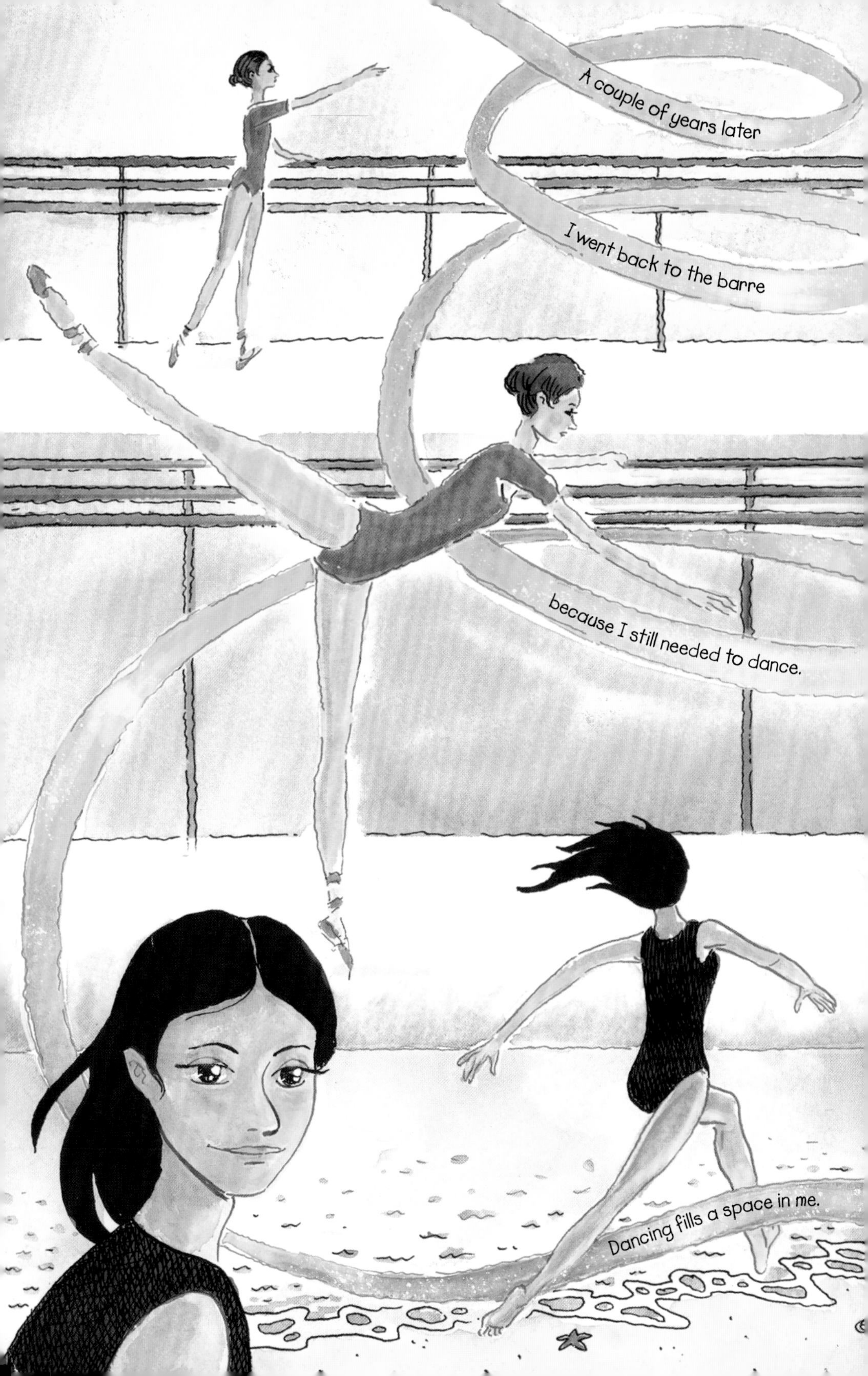
A couple of years later
I went back to the barre
because I still needed to dance.
Dancing fills a space in me.

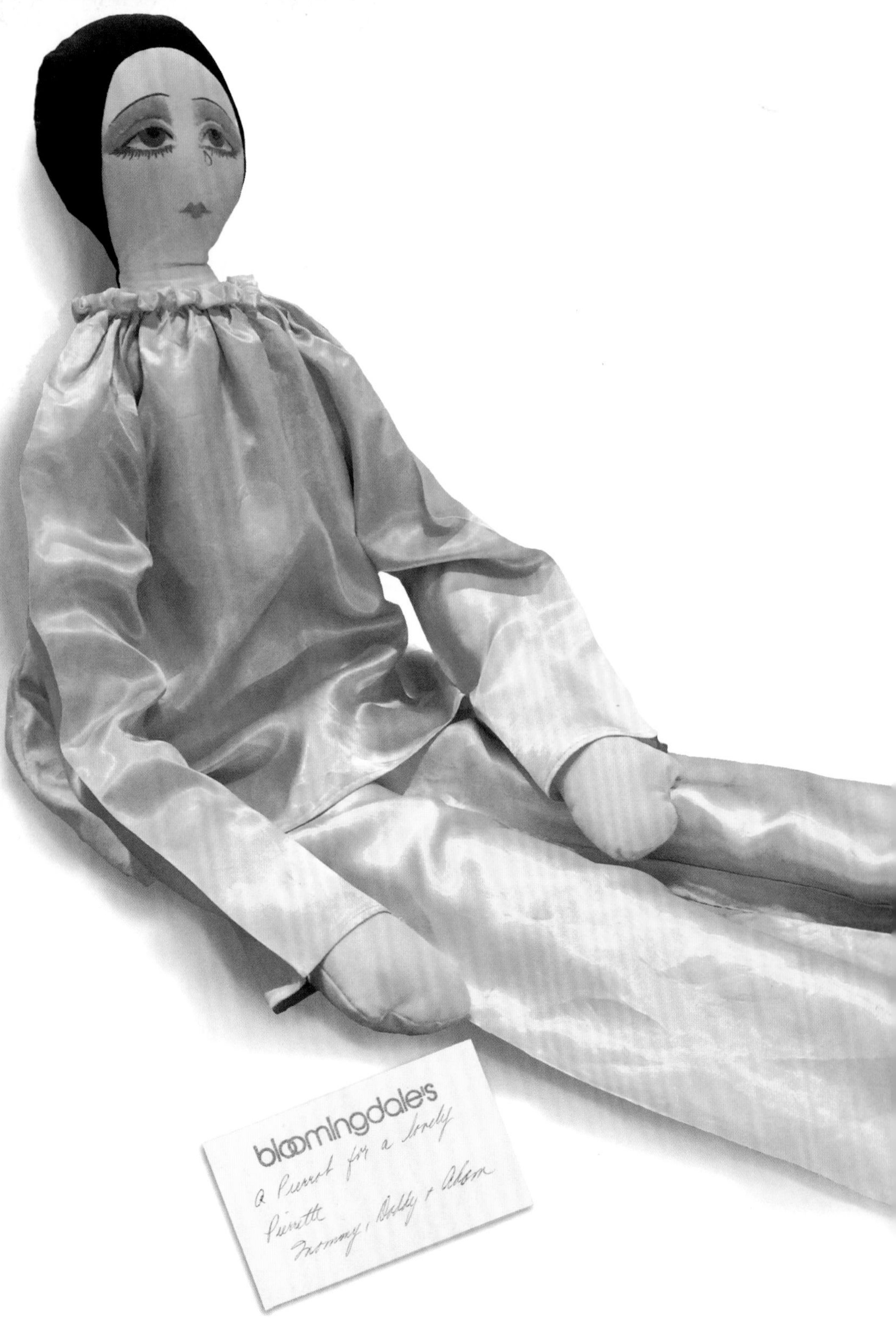
bloomingdale's
a Pierrot for a lovely
Pierrette
Mommy, Daddy + Adam

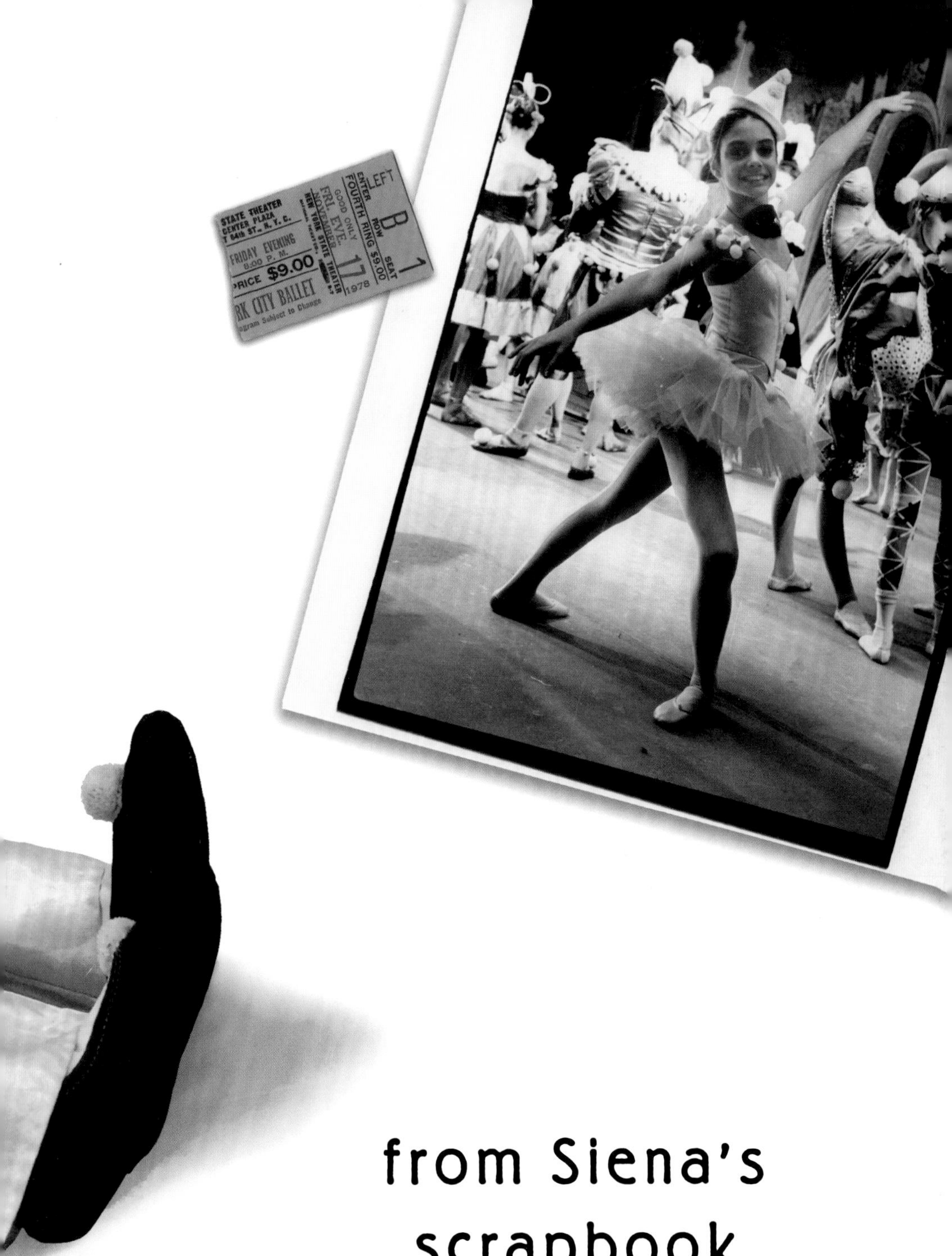
STATE THEATER
CENTER PLAZA
FRIDAY EVENING
8:00 P. M.
PRICE $9.00
LEFT
ENTER
FOURTH RING $9.00
ROW
SEAT
B
1
GOOD ONLY
FRI. EVE.
NOVEMBER
17
1978
NEW YORK STATE THEATER

from Siena's
scrapbook

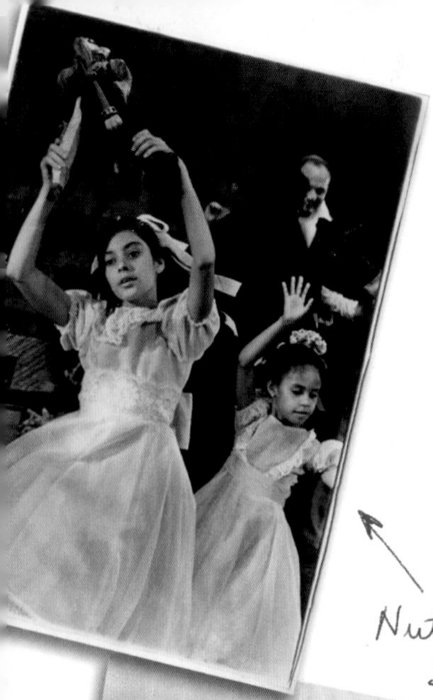

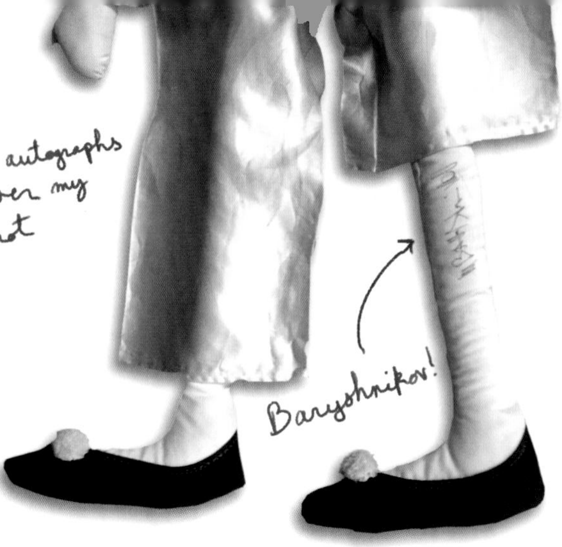

I got autographs all over my Pierrot

Baryshnikov!

Nutcracker performance in San Juan.

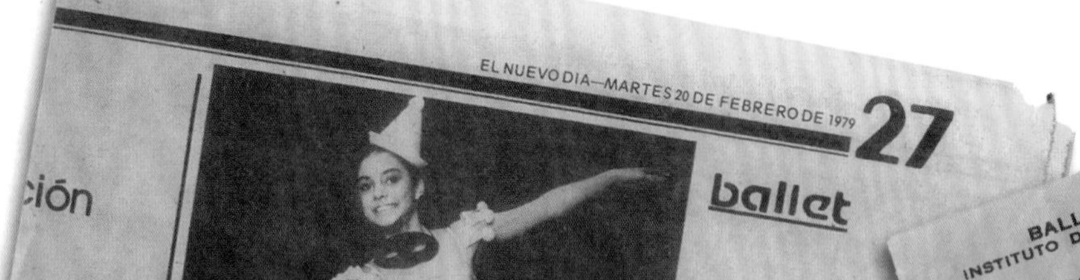

EL NUEVO DIA—MARTES 20 DE FEBRERO DE 1979 27

ción

la noche, será la
chie Torres, en la
posición consta de
la sala Oller de la

952. Tomó sus pri-
Carola Colom Co-
uy joven en varias
o su cuarto año, se
el maestro Rafael
e Greenwich Villa-

eció una beca para
artista regrese a
el círculo artístico
ido ya varias expo-
y otros pueblos de
ica, Museo de Arte
d Católica, Recinto
Padín y la Galería
chas exposiciones
o exposiciones en
y Venezuela.
rse como impre-
ntillano. Es cos-
obra tiene sabor
tros campos y
al para pinta
r las campiña

ballet

En el New York City Ballet

Siena Cherson, quien estudió en la escuela de los Ballets de San Juan, ha estado apareciendo en la producción de los ballets "Coppelia", "Cascanueces" y "Herlequinade" del New York City Ballet en Lincoln Center, bajo la dirección de George Ballanchine, y con la participación de los bailarines Mikhail Baryhnikov, Peter Martins, Peter McBride y Suzanne Farrell. La presente temporada termina esta semana.

de tv

7:05
Deportes con Talo Rivera (6)

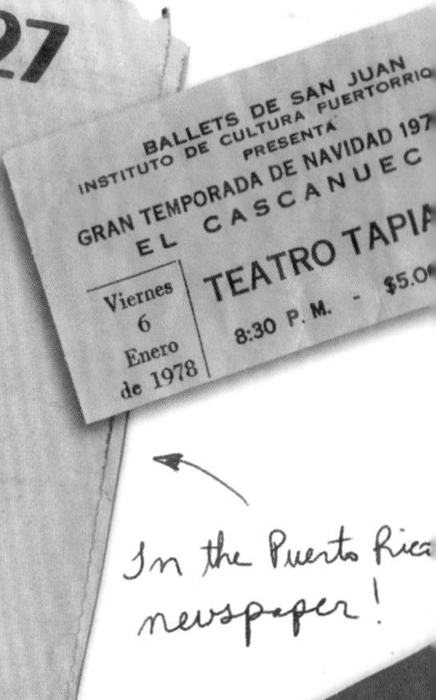

BALLETS DE SAN JUAN
INSTITUTO DE CULTURA PUERTORRIQ
PRESENTA
GRAN TEMPORADA DE NAVIDAD 197
EL CASCANUEC
Viernes 6 Enero de 1978
TEATRO TAPIA
8:30 P.M. - $5.0

In the Puerto Rico newspaper!

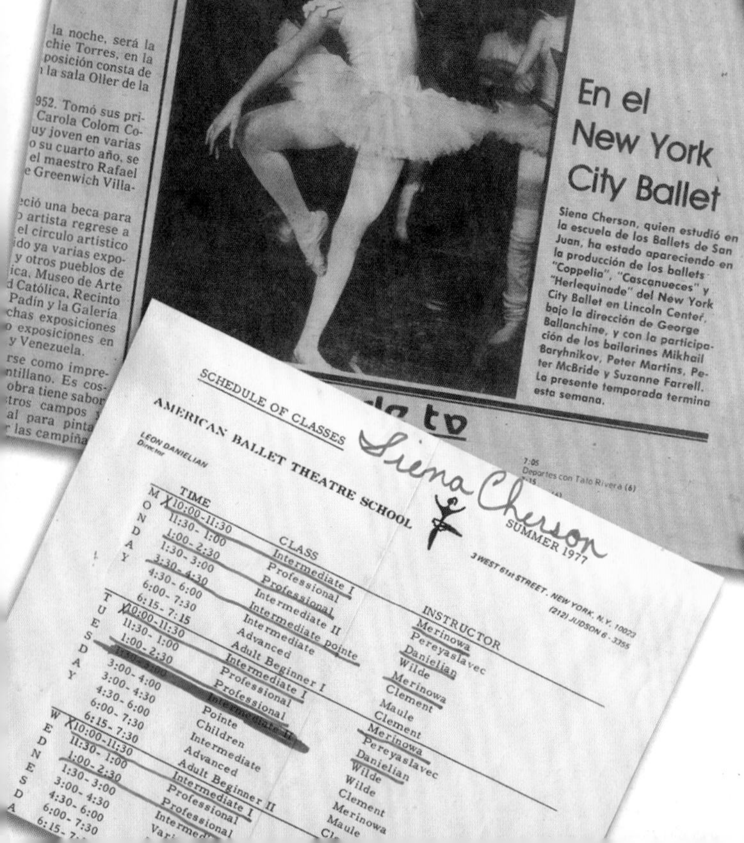

SCHEDULE OF CLASSES
AMERICAN BALLET THEATRE SCHOOL
LEON DANIELIAN
Director
Siena Cherson
SUMMER 1977
3 WEST 61st STREET, NEW YORK, N.Y. 10023
(212) JUDSON 6 - 3355

	TIME	CLASS	INSTRUCTOR
MONDAY	10:00-11:30	Intermediate I	Merinowa
	11:30- 1:00	Professional	Pereyaslavec
	1:00- 2:30	Professional	Danielian
	1:30- 3:00	Intermediate II	Wilde
	3:30- 4:30	Intermediate pointe	Merinowa
	4:30- 6:00	Intermediate	Clement
	6:00- 7:30	Advanced	Maule
	6:15- 7:15	Adult Beginner I	Clement
TUESDAY	10:00-11:30	Intermediate I	Merinowa
	11:30- 1:00	Professional	Pereyaslavec
	1:00- 2:30	Professional	Danielian
		Intermediate II	Wilde
	3:00- 4:00	Pointe	Clement
	3:00- 4:30	Children	Merinowa
	4:30- 6:00	Intermediate	Maule
	6:00- 7:30	Advanced	
	6:15- 7:30	Adult Beginner II	
WEDNESDA	10:00-11:30	Intermediate I	
	11:30- 1:00	Professional	
	1:00- 2:30	Professional	
	1:30- 3:00	Intermed	
	3:00- 4:30	Vari	
	4:30- 6:00		
	6:00- 7:30		
	6:15- 7:		

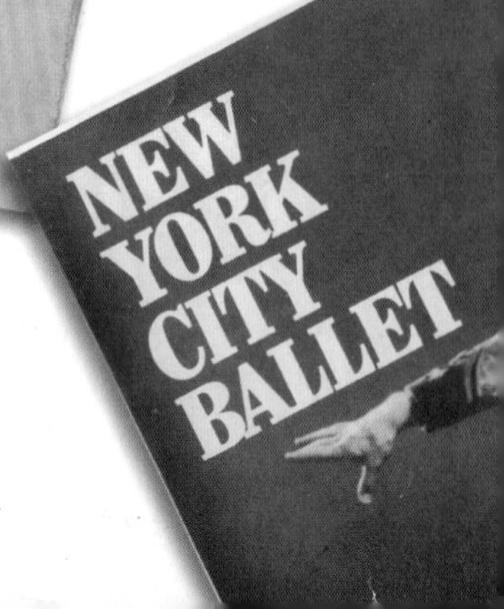
NEW YORK CITY BALLET

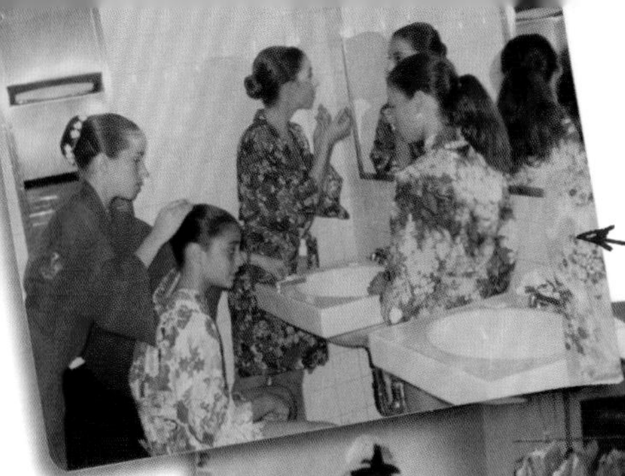

Backstage in our Japanese robes

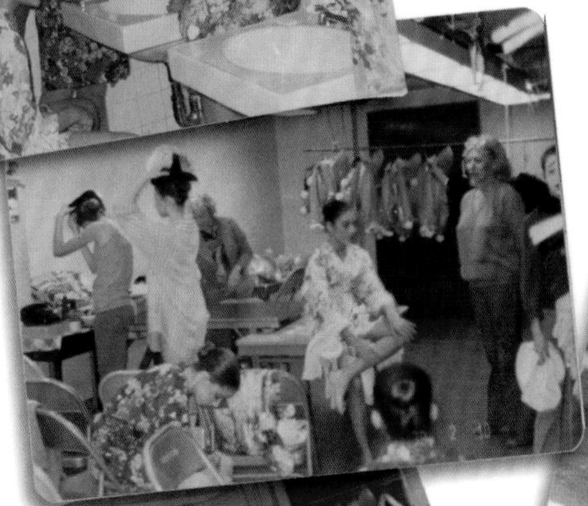

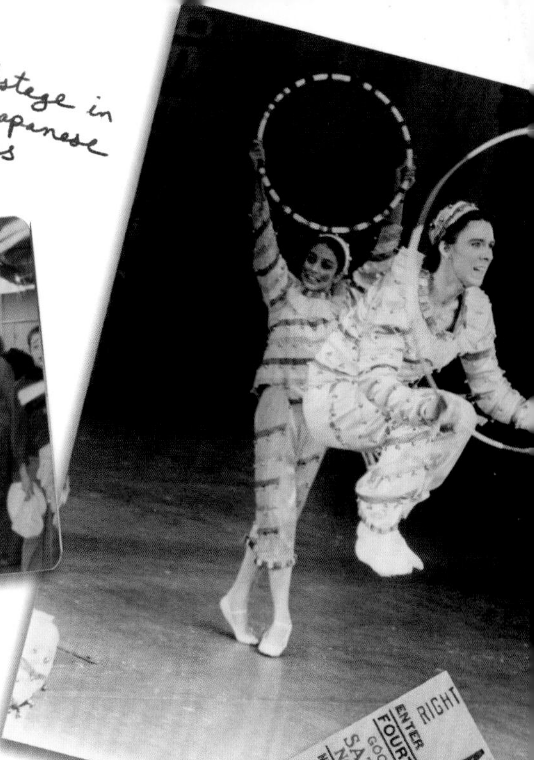

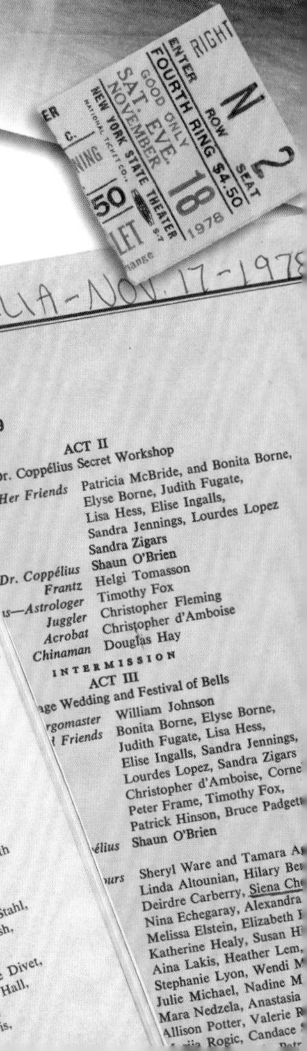
RIGHT
ENTER FOURTH RING
ROW N
SEAT 2
GOOD ONLY SAT. EVE. NOVEMBER 18
1978
NEW YORK STATE THEATER
$4.50

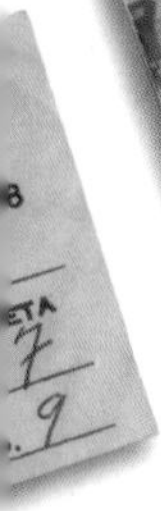

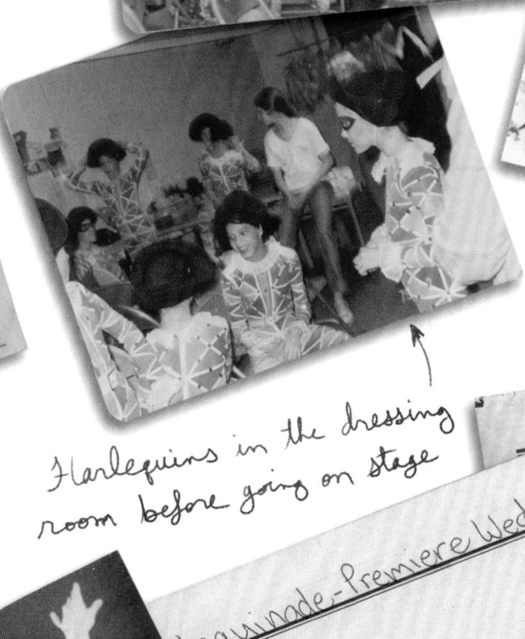

Harlequins in the dressing room before going on stage

COPPÉLIA - NOV. 17 - 1978

n page 39

ACT II

Dr. Coppélius Secret Workshop

a and Her Friends Patricia McBride, and Bonita Borne, Elyse Borne, Judith Fugate, Lisa Hess, Elise Ingalls, Sandra Jennings, Lourdes Lopez Sandra Zigars

Dr. Coppélius Shaun O'Brien

Frantz Helgi Tomasson

s—Astrologer Timothy Fox

Juggler Christopher Fleming

Acrobat Christopher d'Amboise

Chinaman Douglas Hay

INTERMISSION

ACT III

age Wedding and Festival of Bells

rgomaster William Johnson

l Friends Bonita Borne, Elyse Borne, Judith Fugate, Lisa Hess, Elise Ingalls, Sandra Jennings, Lourdes Lopez, Sandra Zigars Christopher d'Amboise, Corne Peter Frame, Timothy Fox, Patrick Hinson, Bruce Padgett

élius Shaun O'Brien

urs Sheryl Ware and Tamara A Linda Altounian, Hilary Be Deirdre Carberry, Siena Ch Nina Echegaray, Alexandra Melissa Elstein, Elizabeth Katherine Healy, Susan H Aina Lakis, Heather Lem, Stephanie Lyon, Wendi M Julie Michael, Nadine M Mara Nedzela, Anastasia Allison Potter, Valerie R Rogic, Candace

-lequinade - Premiere Wed. Nov. 22 1978

ued from page 42

ACT II

An Enchanted Park

arlequin, Colombine, Pierrot, Pierrette, Les Sbires, Cassandre, Léandre, Les Scaramouches, La Bonne Fée, joined by

Ballabile des enfants:

Polichinelles Tamara Molina-Aquire, Hilary Berlind, Maya Ciarrochi, Melissa Elstein, Katherine Healy, Aina Lakis, Heather Lem, Natalie Porat

Les Petits Harlequins Nina Echegaray, Alexandra Ehrlich, Susan Hilferty, Wendi Maguire, Julie Michael, Nadine Miral, Lisa Peters, Maria Rogic

Pierrots et Pierrettes Linda Altounian, Diedre Carberry, Siena Cherson, Julie Keisman, Diane Paulus, Danielle Tiletnick, Julie Tobiason, Katherine Weymouth

Scaramouches Betsy Cooper, Allison Potter, Julie Ronsenbluth, Stephanie Rothenberger, Amy Stahl, Patricia Tomlinson, Tara Walsh, Kim Weild

ités Heléne Alexopoulos, Carole Divet, Susan Freedman, Victoria Hall, Hauser, Lisa Hess, Dana Lewis,

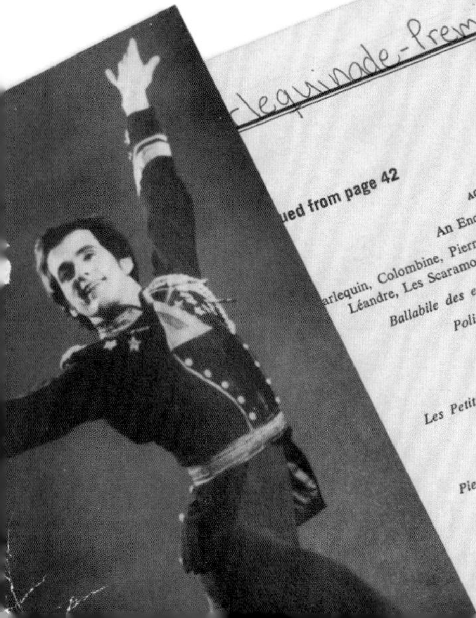

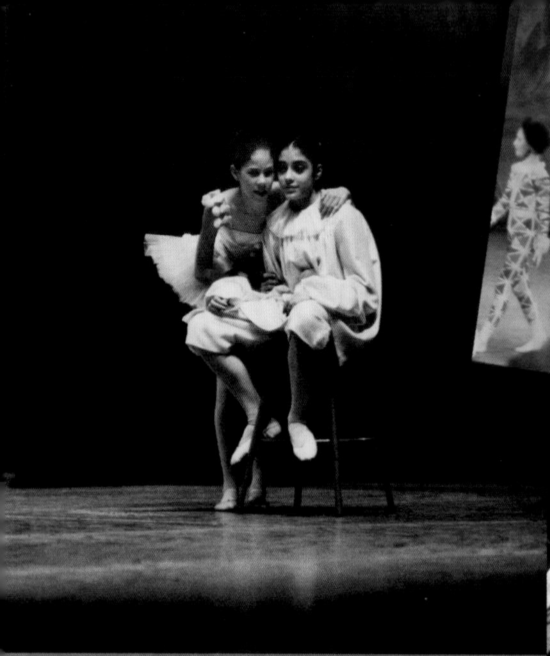

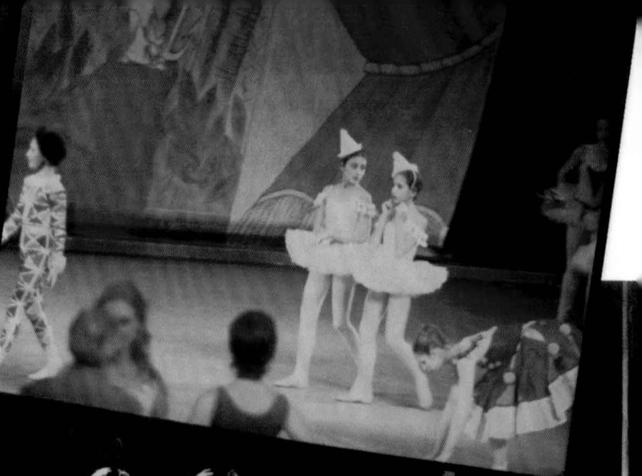

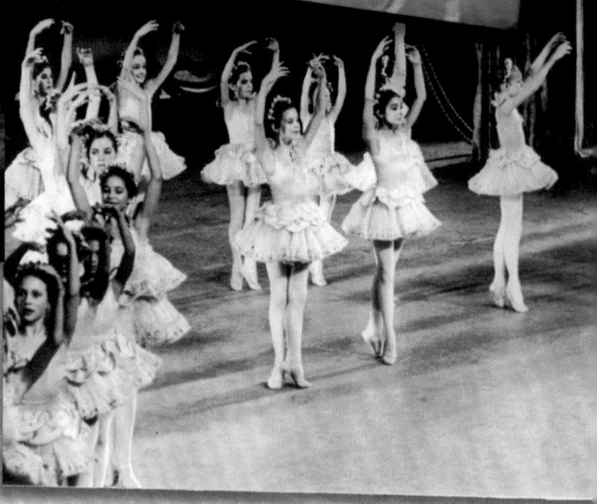

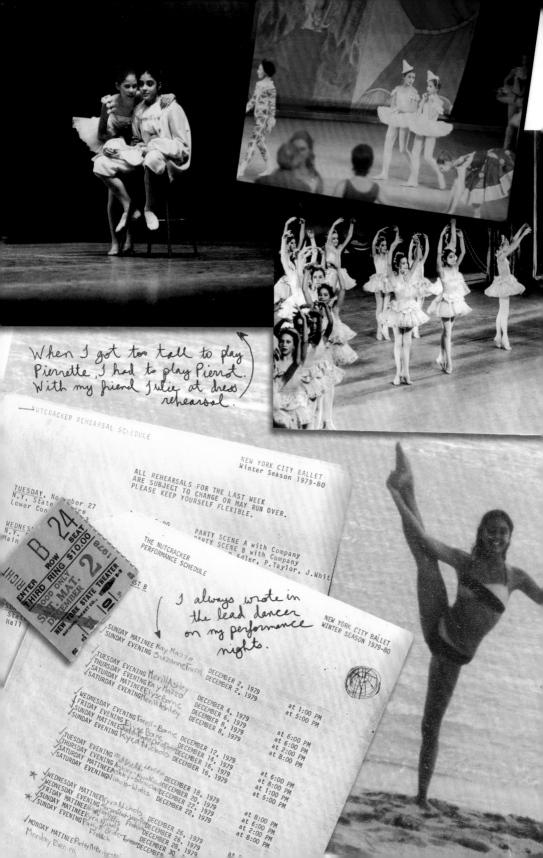

When I got too tall to play Pierrette, I had to play Pierrot. With my friend Julie at dress rehearsal.

NUTCRACKER REHEARSAL SCHEDULE

NEW YORK CITY BALLET
Winter Season 1979-80

ALL REHEARSALS FOR THE LAST WEEK
ARE SUBJECT TO CHANGE OR MAY RUN OVER.
PLEASE KEEP YOURSELF FLEXIBLE.

TUESDAY, No...mber 27
N.Y. State ...tre
Lower Con...

WEDNES...
N.Y. ...
Main ...

PARTY SCENE A with Company
PARTY SCENE B with Company
...Adler, P.Taylor, J.Whit...

RIGHT
ENTER B ROW 24 SEAT
THIRD RING $10.00
GOOD ONLY SAT. MAT. DECEMBER 2 1978
NEW YORK STATE THEATER
NATIONAL TICKET CO.

THE NUTCRACKER
PERFORMANCE SCHEDULE

NEW YORK CITY BALLET
WINTER SEASON 1979-80

I always wrote in the lead dancer on my performance nights.

✓SUNDAY MATINEE Kay Mazzo DECEMBER 2, 1979 at 1:00 PM
✓SUNDAY EVENING Suzanne Farrell DECEMBER 2, 1979 at 5:00 PM

✓TUESDAY EVENING Merill Ashley DECEMBER 4, 1979 at 6:00 PM
✓THURSDAY EVENING Kay Mazzo DECEMBER 6, 1979 at 6:00 PM
✓SATURDAY MATINEE Elyse Borne DECEMBER 8, 1979 at 2:00 PM
✓SATURDAY EVENING Merill Ashley DECEMBER 8, 1979 at 8:00 PM

✓WEDNESDAY EVENING Farell-Bonnie DECEMBER 12, 1979 at 6:00 PM
✓FRIDAY EVENING Elyse Borne DECEMBER 14, 1979 at 8:00 PM
✓SUNDAY MATINEE Judith Fugate DECEMBER 16, 1979 at 1:00 PM
✓SUNDAY EVENING Kyra Nichols DECEMBER 16, 1979 at 5:00 PM

✓TUESDAY EVENING McBride-Lavery DECEMBER 18, 1979 at 8:00 PM
✓THURSDAY EVENING Ashley-Kyra Nichols DECEMBER 20, 1979 at 6:00 PM
✓SATURDAY MATINEE Ashley-Stravinsky DECEMBER 22, 1979 at 2:00 PM
✓SATURDAY EVENING Nichols-Watts DECEMBER 22, 1979 at 8:00 PM

*✓WEDNESDAY MATINEE Kyra Nichols DECEMBER 26, 1979
✓WEDNESDAY EVENING Susan Gluck-Jean-Pierre DECEMBER 26, 1979
✓FRIDAY MATINEE Nichols-Watts Frohlich DECEMBER 28, 1979
*✓SUNDAY MATINEE Kyra Nichols DECEMBER 30, 1979
✓SUNDAY EVENING Patty McBride-Frohlich DECEMBER 30, 1979

✓MONDAY MATINEE Patty McBride-... DECEMBER ...
Monday Evening

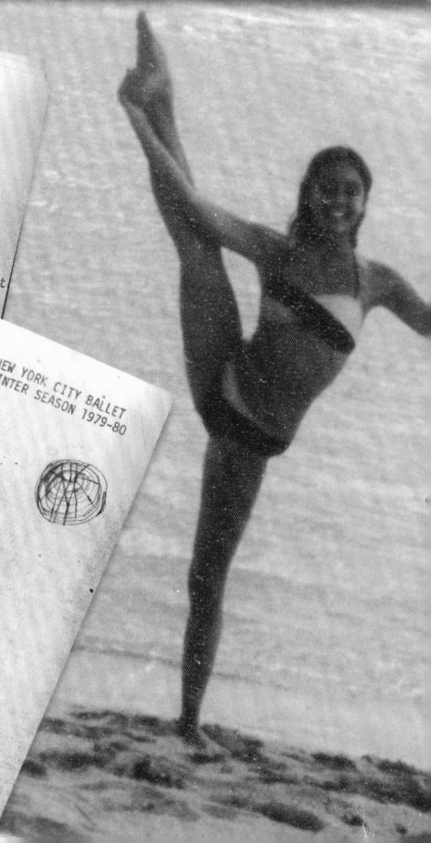

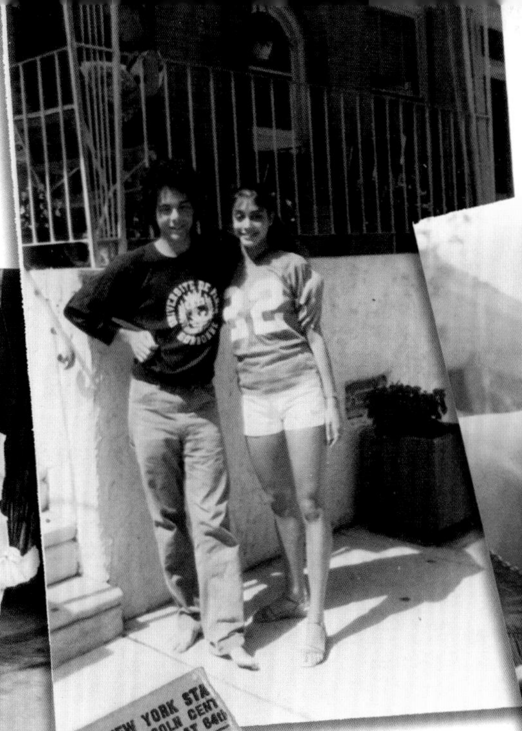

With Adam in my favorite Miami Dolphins jersey.

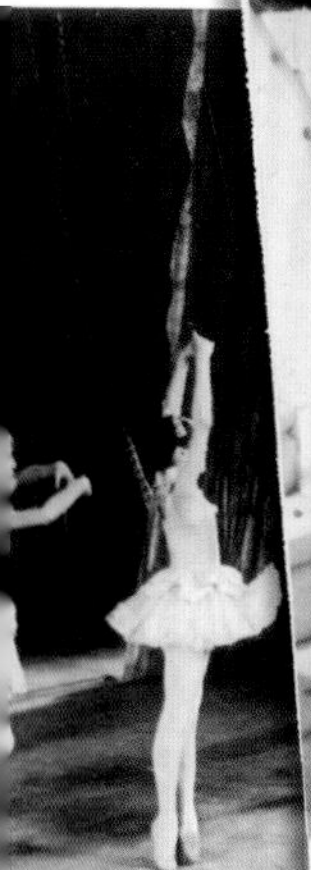

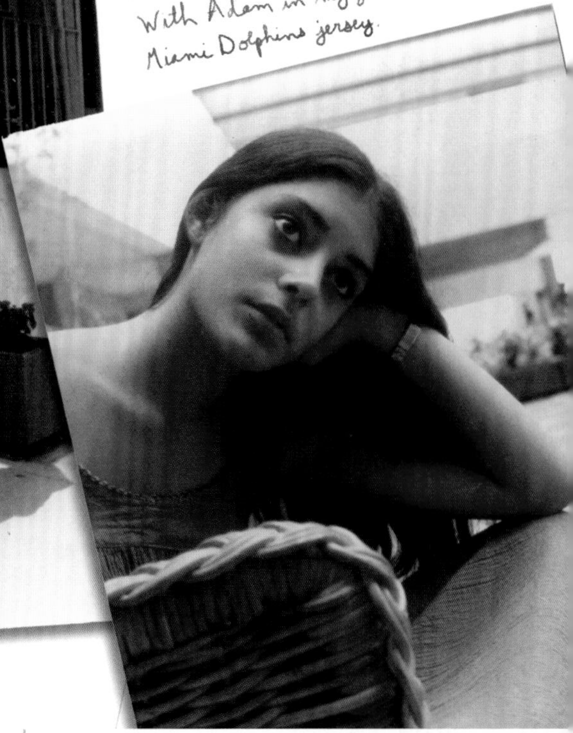

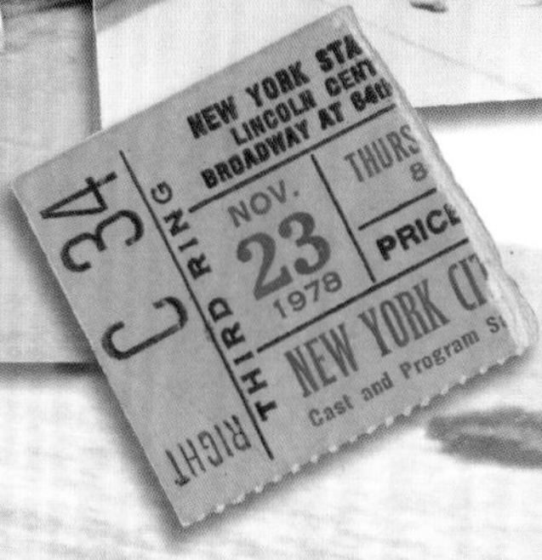
NEW YORK STA
LINCOLN CENT
BROADWAY AT 64
THURS
NOV.
23
1978
PRICE
C 34
THIRD RING
RIGHT
NEW YORK CI
Cast and Program S

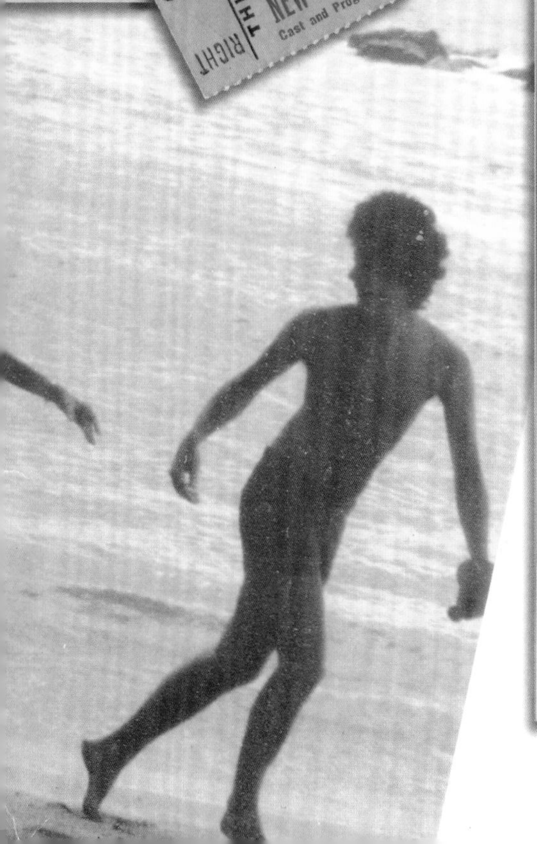

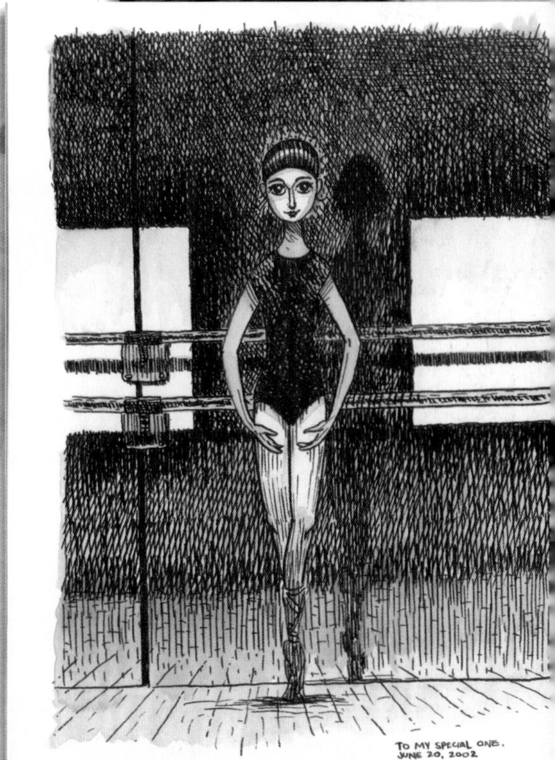
TO MY SPECIAL ONE.
JUNE 20, 2002

Mark's first study for "To Dance"!

ATHENEUM BOOKS FOR YOUNG READERS

An imprint of Simon & Schuster Children's Publishing Division

1230 Avenue of the Americas, New York, New York 10020

This work is a memoir. It reflects the author's present recollections
of her experiences over a period of years.

For information about special discounts for bulk purchases, please contact Simon & Schuster Special Sales at
1-866-506-1949 or business@simonandschuster.com.

The Simon & Schuster Speakers Bureau can bring authors to your live event.

For more information or to book an event, contact the Simon & Schuster Speakers Bureau
at 1-866-248-3049 or visit our website at www.simonspeakers.com.

Also available in an Atheneum Books for Young Readers paperback edition

Book design by Mark Siegel

The text for this book was set in Lemonade and Housepaint.

The illustrations for this book were rendered in watercolor and ink.

Manufactured in China

0719 SCP

First Edition

10 9 8 7 6 5 4 3 2 1

CIP data for this book is available from the Library of Congress.

ISBN 978-1-4814-8663-7 (hc)

ISBN 978-1-4814-8664-4 (pbk)

ISBN 978-1-4814-8665-1 (eBook)